The LionheART Guide to Formatting

A Self-Publishing Guide for Independent Authors

by

Karen Perkins

LionheART Publishing House

LionheART Publishing House
Harrogate
UK

www.lionheartgalleries.co.uk
www.facebook.com/lionheartpublishing
publishing@lionheartgalleries.co.uk

First published in Great Britain in 2014 by
LionheART Publishing House
Copyright © Karen Perkins 2014, 2015
ISBN: 978-1-910115-04-6

Classification: Editing, Formatting, Indie, Self-Publishing, Writing,
Publishing, Guides, Self-Help

Cover Design by CC Morgan Creative Visuals

Contents

Introduction

The LionheART Guide to Formatting is a companion guide to *The LionheART Guide to Editing Fiction* and is a comprehensive, step-by-step guide to formatting e-book and paperback manuscripts in Word.

I format approximately a hundred books a year and *The LionheART Guide to Formatting* explains in a simple and clear manner how to format your manuscript for publishing, plus how to upload your finalised files to the most popular sites: Kindle Direct Publishing, Smashwords, and CreateSpace.

A reader should not be able to tell whether a book has been published independently or traditionally just by reading it – and quite simply, they also deserve a self-published book to be of the same high standard as a book from one of the major publishing houses. This means getting all the elements right – not just the story, but also the editing, formatting and cover.

There are two options for getting the formatting right: hiring a formatter or learning to do it yourself. This guide is for authors who want to be intimately involved (and in control) of every aspect of their book. I wanted to compile a reference tool which is simple, easy to use and full of tips to help you.

If you prefer to spend your time writing, LionheART Publishing House offers a range of high-quality, low-cost publishing services, full details of which are on the website: www.lionheartgalleries.co.uk

*

As writers we are wordsmiths, creating a world, characters and story with language, and punctuation is one of the tools of language. To ignore it, except for rare exceptions, to me is like Monet painting with badly mixed colours, or Michelangelo attempting to sculpt using a hammer when a chisel is needed.

Words are what we do, language is our medium and punctuation is our tool. When I write, I want to take my readers to my world, to join my characters on their journey, to experience their challenges, traumas and desires. I want them to take this journey with me, without noticing the individual words, full stops or commas. I want them to lose themselves in the story, not in the mechanics of it, and this will only happen if all the elements are right.

Karen Perkins
LionheART Publishing House
www.lionheartgalleries.co.uk

The LionheART Guide to Formatting

Generic Formatting

Formatting for e-books is not straightforward. What you see in Word will not necessarily be what the reader sees on their device. There are a multitude of e-readers out there – Kindle, Nook and Kobo are the most popular, along with iPads, iPods and other tablets and smartphones. Within each brand there are a number of options, for example at the time of writing there are ten different Kindles alone available, each with a multitude of possible settings: font size, line spacing, margins, colour and screen rotation. An incorrectly formatted e-book, e.g. with extra spaces at the end of a paragraph, line breaks instead of paragraph breaks, extra paragraph breaks or tabs can result in blank lines and blank pages to interfere with your readers' experience.

In a well-formatted book, readers will not notice the formatting, allowing them to lose themselves in your story. Tidying up these areas will not only result in an excellent e-book but also a professionally presented paperback. This will not only attract readers, but also help you gain good reviews, and help you build a strong author brand.

Before you start, go to the 'Review' tab in Word, and ensure no changes are still being tracked by clicking on 'Accept all changes and stop tracking' and delete any editing comments that remain in your manuscript.

1. Formatting Marks

The first step is to show the formatting marks – line breaks, tabs, paragraph breaks etc. To enable this function, click on the "Home" tab on the toolbar in Word, then click on the "Show/Hide" button (the paragraph break symbol shown below) positioned in the centre of the toolbar.

tibility Mo

Add-Ins

¶

This will show every formatting mark in your manuscript, including spaces between the words. As indie-publishers our largest market is usually e-books, in particular Kindle, and it's important to understand how the formatting tools you use affect the end result, for example using paragraph breaks rather than line breaks, making sure there are no extra paragraph breaks (which may result in blank pages in the final e-book), no extra spaces, and no tabs etc.

Line break symbol: "Shift" and "Enter".

This will split a line, keeping the justification, without any indentation so the text flows.

Paragraph break symbol: "Ctrl" and "Enter".

This will start a new paragraph, so the last line of the previous paragraph will not fill the previous line, and the new paragraph will start with the indent set (see the chapter on Formatting Text, Including Indents)

Tab symbol:

Space symbol:

The easiest way to tidy up your formatting marks is by using the "Find and Replace" function on the "Home" toolbar and positioned at the far right-hand side, and there are a number of searches I do on every file before moving ahead with the format.

i. Removing Extra Spaces Between Words

Click on "Replace", move your cursor to the "Find What" box, delete anything that is already in there, then depress the space bar twice.

Move your cursor to the "Replace With" box, delete anything that is already in there, then depress the space bar once.

Click "Replace All".

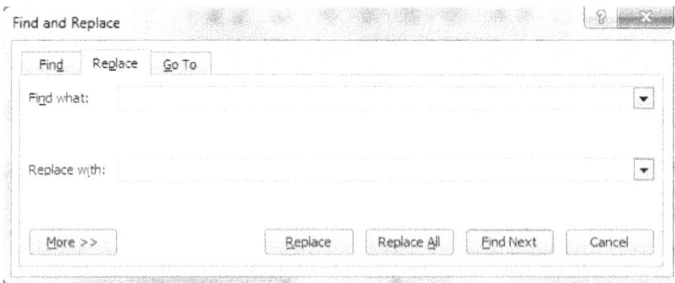

You will then see a box telling you how many replacements have been made. If this is "0", click "OK" and move on to the next item in the list. If there is any other figure in this box, click "OK", then "Replace

All" again. Keep doing this until your result is zero replacements.

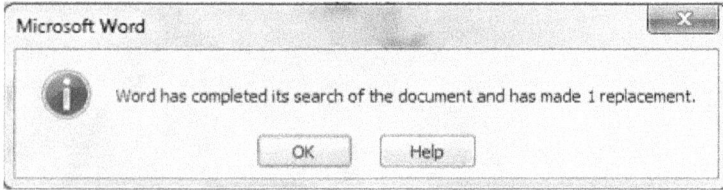

Microsoft Word

Word has completed its search of the document and has made 1 replacement.

OK   Help

ii. Replacing Line Breaks with Paragraph Breaks

You can search for formatting marks by using their caret codes. The caret is the "American Standard Code for Information Interchange", it is the symbol ^ and is found by pressing "shift" and "6".

The caret code for a line break is ^l and for a paragraph break ^p.

Type ^l into the "Find What" box, and ^p into the "Replace With" box as follows.

Find and Replace

Find   Replace   Go To

Find what: ^l

Replace with: ^p

More >>   Replace   Replace All   Find Next   Cancel

Click on "Replace All", then "OK" when the replacements (if any) have been made.

iii. Ellipses

The correct format for an ellipsis is to use spaces before and between the three dots (*always* three), as well as a space afterwards if the narrative or dialogue continues . . .

There is no space at the end when it forms the end of a paragraph or is closed by quotation/speech marks, nor is there a further full stop, comma or exclamation mark, although occasionally a question mark can be used. Using this format with spaces gives the best look to a paperback book, allowing the justification of the text to be well balanced. It is especially important for e-readers as you cannot dictate where a line will end. If you don't put a space before the ellipsis, it can look like a full stop, followed by a couple of dots on the next line. Leaving out the spaces between the dots connects two words and pushes the line out of balance.

If you have used any other format than the one above in your manuscript, the easiest way to replace them is to select the ellipsis in your text, copy it ("ctrl" and "c"), paste into the "Find what" box, then enter " . . . " without the quotation/speech marks (space dot space dot space dot space) in the "Replace With" box and click "Replace All". For some reason, just putting the dots in the "Find What" box, even in exactly the same format you have used in your manuscript, does not always work.

The next step is to format those instances where quotation/speech marks directly follow the ellipsis. The step we have just carried out above inserts an extra space before the closing quotation/speech mark. Enter the new format of ellipsis followed by a quotation/speech mark (. . . " or . . . ' as appropriate) into the "Find What" box, then repeat it in the "Replace With" box, omitting the space between the last dot and the closing quotation/speech mark.

iv. Removing Extra Spaces From the Ends and Beginnings of Paragraphs

In "Find What" put in a space then ^p

In "Replace With", enter ^p without the space.

Click "Replace All".

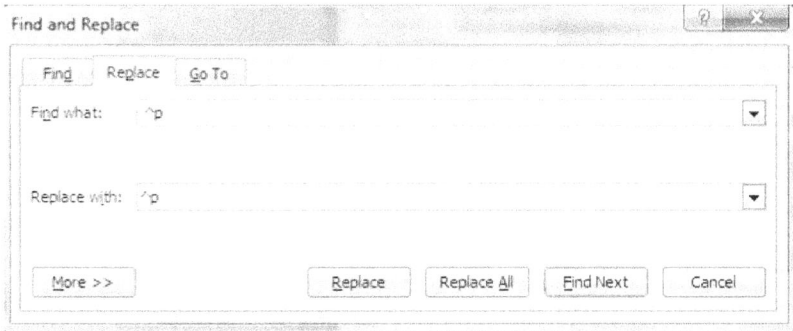

Keep doing this replacement until your result is zero – all the extra spaces at the ends of your paragraphs have now been removed.

Then repeat using a space following ^p in the "Find What" box, which will clear erroneous spaces at the beginning of your paragraphs, keeping your indentation consistent.

v. Removing Tabs

The caret code for a tab is ^t

In "Find What" enter ^t

Delete anything in the "Replace With" box and leave it empty.

Click "Replace All".

As e-readers cannot use tabs, this also means that automatic lists, whether numbered or with bullet points, are not available to use when creating an e-book, and need to be numbered by hand, or an asterisk used instead of bullet points.

If you have used tabs to indent your paragraphs, see the chapter on formatting text, including indents.

vi. Smart Quotes

There are two styles of quotation/speech marks, straight: ' " and smart: ' ". Smart quotes add more professionalism to your book and you can set Word to automatically replace straight quotes with smart quotes:

First, go to "File" and click on "Options" near the bottom:

then click on "Proofing":

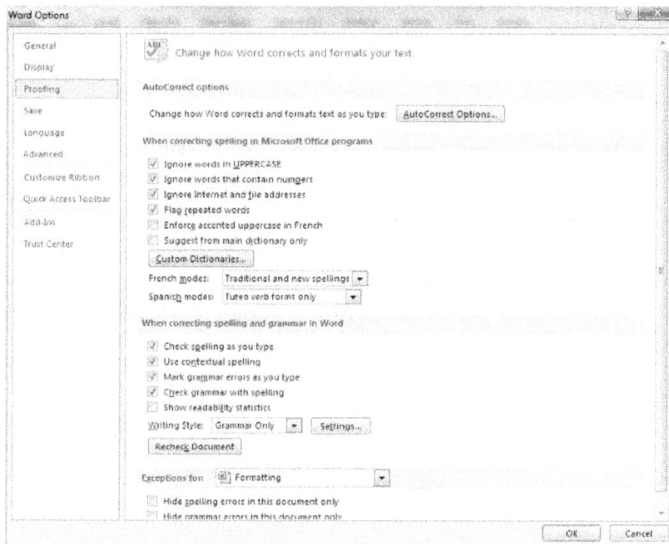

Next, click on "AutoCorrect Options", then on the "AutoFormat" tab:

Untick all the boxes except "Replace "Straight Quotes" with "Smart Quotes"" and the two "Preserve" boxes as above. Click "OK", then click on the "AutoFormat As You Type" tab.

On this screen, untick all the boxes except ""Straight Quotes" with "Smart Quotes"", then "OK".

Removing all the other auto-formatting options at this stage will help to prevent problems when you come to do your Smashwords/EPUB format – but more about that later.

2. Headers and Footers

Delete any headers, footers and/or page numbers from the file. They will not convert to e-books and can cause problems, especially with Smashwords, and you format them correctly for the paperback when you come to do that format – there are a few other steps to do first.

To delete headers, point your cursor at the header and right click, you will then have a box giving you the option to "Edit Header". Clicking on this gives you access to the header, which you select and delete.

Next, move to the bottom of the file and do the same to any footer/page numbers, then close the "Header and Footer Tools" tab on the toolbar.

3. Formatting Text, Including Indents

Many authors use the tab button or a number of spaces to indent their paragraphs, but this will result in a badly formatted e-book. E-readers cannot use these formatting tools, and your indentations in the final e-book will be excessive and inconsistent.

Instead, assign your full manuscript to the "Normal" style – although this may have happened automatically depending on which version of Word you are using. If so, you will still need to modify the "Normal" style.

The style tools are under the "Home" tab on the right-hand half of the toolbar:

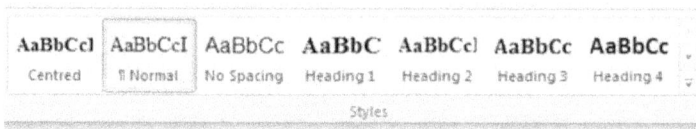

AaBbCcI	AaBbCcI	AaBbCc	AaBbC	AaBbCcI	AaBbCc	AaBbCc
Centred	¶ Normal	No Spacing	Heading 1	Heading 2	Heading 3	Heading 4

Styles

If a style is already assigned to your text, its box will be highlighted in yellow. If nothing is highlighted, select the whole of your document (by pressing "ctrl" and "a"), then right click on the "Normal" style box, which will give you the following options:

AaBbCcI AaBbCc **AaBbC** AaBbCcI

Norm

Update Normal to Match Selection

Modify...

Select All: (No Data)

Rename...

Remove from Quick Style Gallery

hors use

nstead, a

Add Gallery to Quick Access Toolbar

Click on "Modify", which brings up the following box:

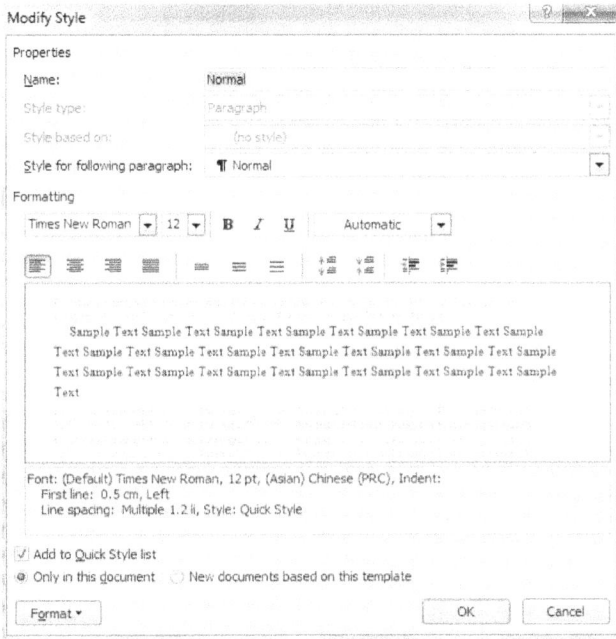

Modify Style

Properties

Name: Normal

Style type: Paragraph

Style based on: (no style)

Style for following paragraph: ¶ Normal

Formatting

Times New Roman   12   **B** *I* U   Automatic

Sample Text Sample Text

Font: (Default) Times New Roman, 12 pt, (Asian) Chinese (PRC), Indent:
   First line: 0.5 cm, Left
   Line spacing: Multiple 1.2 li, Style: Quick Style

☑ Add to Quick Style list
◉ Only in this document   ○ New documents based on this template

Format ▼   OK   Cancel

Here you will set the parameters for setting out your manuscript, which is very useful to prepare the common formatting elements between the Kindle, EPUB (usually Smashwords) and paperback formats – again saving you time and lessening the potential for formatting errors in your final files.

Always set the font to Times New Roman – this is the only font the e-readers can all handle (although you are free to use whichever font you wish for your paperbacks, as long as you hold the correct licence) – and set the size to 11 or 12 depending on your style of book and personal preference. Then ensure the bold, italics and underlining buttons are not enabled, and the font colour is set to "Automatic".

Clicking on "Format" at the left-hand bottom corner will give you a list of options:

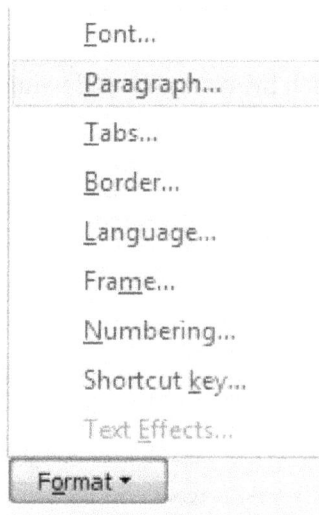

Font...

Paragraph...

Tabs...

Border...

Language...

Frame...

Numbering...

Shortcut key...

Text Effects...

Format ▾

Click on "Paragraph" to bring up the next dialogue box and complete it as follows:

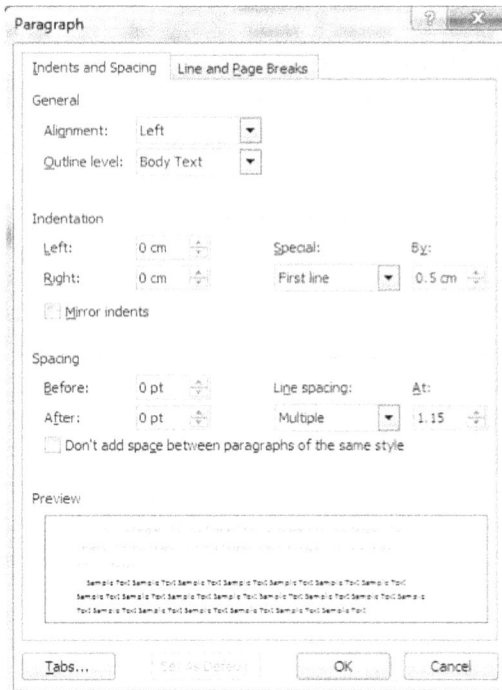

Alignment: Left
Outline Levels: Body Text
Indentation:
Left: 0 cm
Right: 0 cm
Special: First Line 0.5 cm
Spacing:
Before: 0 pt
After: 0 pt
Line Spacing: Multiple 1.15

Click "OK", which takes you back to the previous dialogue box. Click "OK" here as well to go back to your manuscript.

If you are preparing your manuscript for submission to agents rather than self-publishing, read their submission requirements carefully and enter the appropriate values at this stage.

4. Page Breaks

The best way to ensure each section or chapter begins on a new page is by using page breaks.

Go to the end of the last paragraph of each chapter in turn (and the end of each of your front and back papers), press "enter" to move the cursor down to the line below your text and press "ctrl" and "enter" together. This inserts a page break (shown below) and takes you to the top of the next page. By placing it on the line below your text, this will not affect the justification in the final book. If you place the page break on the same line of your text, the end result may be a short line spread out over the width of the e-reader or page in your paperback, and if you have a number of paragraph breaks between your text and the page break, this may inadvertently insert a blank page in your e-book.

................................Page Break................................¶

Don't worry if this results in a blank page in your Word document; this is purely due to the page break falling at the top of a new page and will not result in a blank page in your final book. Having said that, it is possible that on certain settings on certain devices, this may happen on an e-reader as well, but unfortunately there is nothing we can do to control where the page ends as an e-book format needs to be so versatile – but it will not occur across all e-readers and/or all settings. If it occurs in your paperback format you can simply delete the page break to solve the problem.

5. Chapter Headings

The next stage is to format your chapter headings, which will make it easier for you to navigate your manuscript as well as insert a table of contents when you come to finalize the formats. An added bonus is that this will give you an easy double-check that your chapters are numbered correctly and consistently.

1. Put an empty paragraph break at the top of your page and have your heading on the second line. This is particularly important for the Kindle format as the conversion to the Kindle file (.MOBI) often loses the centring of your chapter headings and this is the only method I have found to ensure each heading is centred in the final e-book. (*The Smashwords Style Guide* suggests slightly indenting the chapter heading to combat this problem – but this does not work every time.)

2. Select your first heading (whether an item in your front papers, prologue or first chapter) and assign the "Heading 1" style by selecting the heading and clicking on "Heading 1":

AaBbCcl	AaBbCcI	AaBbCcI	**AaBbC**	AaBbCcl	AaBbCc	**AaBbCc**
Centred	¶ Normal	No Spacing	Heading 1	Heading 2	Heading 3	Heading 4

Styles

The next stage is to modify "Heading 1" by right-clicking on it as we did before with "Normal".

Keep the font as Times New Roman, but here use a larger size. My standard is 14 as this looks best on e-readers. Also ensure the font colour is set to "Automatic", which will ensure the text is readable no matter which colour setting your reader is using on their device. By ticking the "Automatically Update" box near the bottom, you can change your heading style later on one heading in the manuscript and it will carry through to all your other headings (although it is always worth double-checking that this has worked). Next click on "Format" then "Paragraph" as before to bring up the second dialogue box:

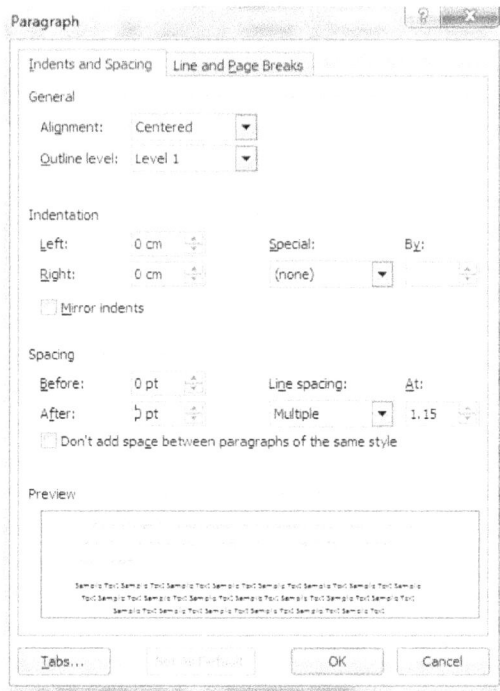

This shows the LionheART standard settings as follows:

Alignment: Centred
Outline Levels: Level 1
Indentation:
Left: 0 cm
Right: 0 cm
Special: None
Spacing:
Before: 0 pt
After: 0 pt
Line Spacing: Multiple 1.15

Click "OK" to close the box and again in the next one.

Select each heading in turn and apply this "Heading 1" by clicking on the box. If your Navigation pane is open on the left-hand side of your screen, click on the left-hand icon and you will see a list of your headings appear:

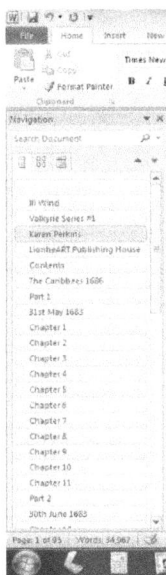

If the navigation pane is not visible, click on "Find" in the top right-hand corner of the toolbar under the "Home" tab, which should bring it up. It is always worth checking this list to make sure no chapters have been missed out and they are numbered correctly and consistently.

Between the chapter heading and the text of the chapter, I recommend inserting two empty lines for presentation, although you can use a single line or none at all if you prefer. Any more than two is too much for the smaller e-readers and can result in empty pages being inserted in the final e-book.

If you have subheadings, assign these to "Heading 2" and set the parameters to your requirements.

Finally, ensure you put a page break at the end of each chapter so that the new chapter will start on a new screen.

6. Block Paragraphs

In e-books, all block paragraphs are marked by an asterisk (or another symbol if you so wish). Some authors prefer to use a number of asterisks, but take care not to use too many. If a reader has a small e-reader set to a large font, using too many asterisks can result in them being spread over more than one line.

Paperbacks only include the asterisk when the block paragraph falls at the end or beginning of a page. By having them in place at this stage, you ensure they will be present in both your e-book formats, and they are easy to spot and amend when you come to do the paperback format.

Also check your indents at the start of each block paragraph, including the start of your chapters. There should be no indent unless the paragraph/chapter starts with dialogue, in which case it is always indented, whether direct dialogue (speech) or indirect (thoughts). To remove the indent, place your cursor at the start of the line, then press backspace.

7. Saving

Save this file as your master copy, then "Save As" new copies, one for each format you will be doing, and make it very clear which is which so that you upload the correct file to each site. E.g. Title MASTER, Title KINDLE, Title CREATESPACE (there is a reason for not saving a Smashwords file at this point, which I explain in the Smashwords/EPUB formatting section).

Save as a .doc file at this stage (Word 97-2003 File), as the docx format can cause corruptions, particularly in Kindle files.

Kindle Formatting

Now that you have completed the generic formatting, open the file you have designated for Kindle. There is not much more to do to this file to get it ready, and the best place to start is the table of contents.

1. Table of Contents

The table of contents goes immediately before your first chapter or prologue. If you have not already done so, go to the appropriate page or use page breaks to create a page for your table of contents. Leave a blank line at the top, then write out the heading (either Contents or Table of Contents) and assign it to "Heading 1".

Insert a couple of empty lines after the heading to match the way you have presented the start of your chapters, then click on the next line to place your table of contents.

Click on the "References" tab on your toolbar, then "Table of Contents" at the left-hand side, then click on "Insert Table of Contents" near the bottom of the dialogue box. (Do not click on one of the automatic tables as this will include page numbers, which you do not want in an e-book. Kindles automatically configure location numbers, percentage read numbers, or time remaining in book.)

In the next dialogue box, below, click on "Modify".

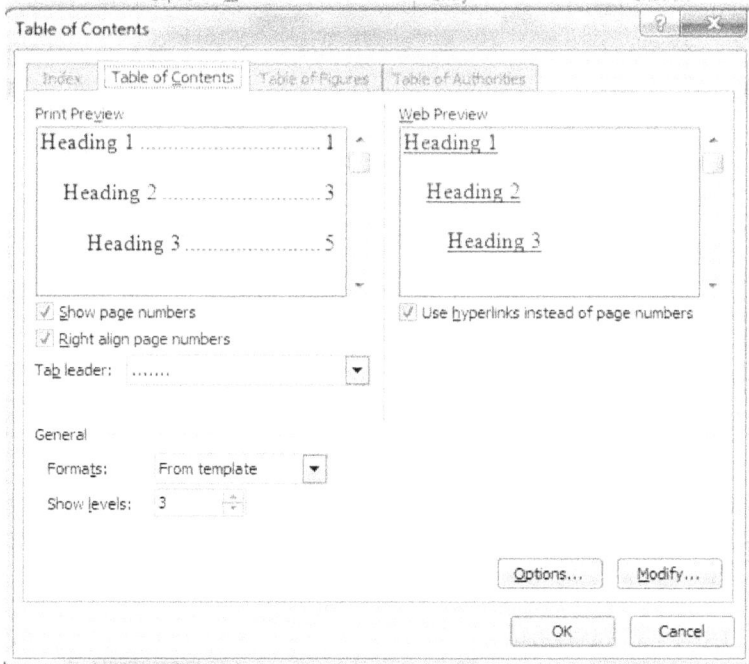

Then on "Modify" again in the next box.

The next box should be familiar to you as it is the same as you used when you modified the Normal and Heading 1 styles:

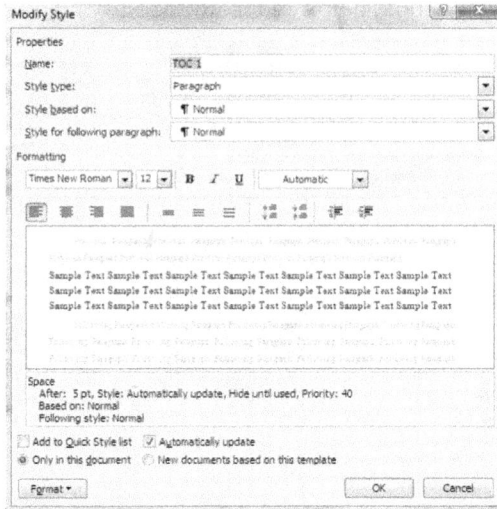

In here, you can choose whether to have your table of contents justified to the left or centred. Personally, I prefer centred for fiction and left justified for non-fiction, especially where there are subheadings, but this is purely your own preference. Next click on "Format", then "Paragraph" as before and set the "Special Indent" to "None":

Also, it is a good idea to add a 5 pt spacing in the "After" box. With so many devices having touch screens now, it is frustrating for readers when the spacing is so close that it is difficult to touch the right chapter and they have to go backwards and forwards to get to the point in the book they are looking for.

Next click "OK" to close this box, then the next and the next until you are back at the following screen.

Untick the boxes for "Show page numbers" and "Right align page numbers", ensure the "Use hyperlinks instead of page numbers" is ticked, then click "OK". Your linked table of contents should now be in place.

You will notice there is an entry within the table labelled "Contents" as in the example below and which needs to be deleted as it will confuse Kindle.

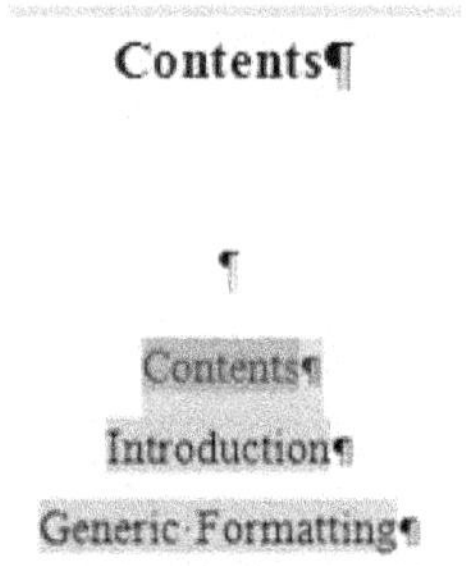

Contents¶

¶

Contents¶

Introduction¶

Generic·Formatting¶

Highlight the entry, taking care that it is only this line that is selected, then press backspace. The table is very sensitive, and if you delete more than you meant to, press "ctrl" and "Z" to undo, and try again.

There is one last job to do before the contents page is ready, and that is to bookmark the contents heading to enable the "Go To Contents" function on Kindles. Select the text (Contents), then go to the "Insert" tab in the toolbar. Click on "Bookmark" (in the centre of the bar) and you will see this screen:

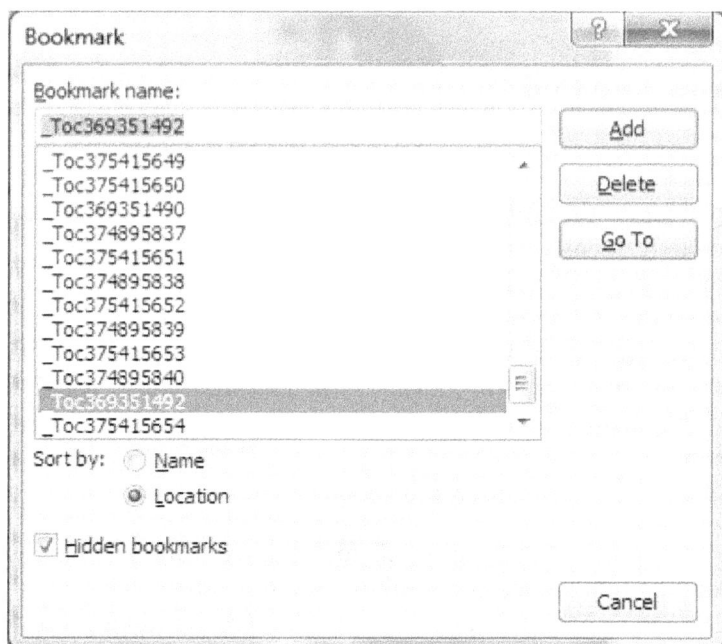

The entries you see here are the links between the table of contents and your chapters. Replace the highlighted entry in the "Bookmark Name" box with "ref_toc" (omitting the speech marks) and click "Add". The box will close and your table of contents is now fully linked.

2. Front and End Matter

The placing of the front and end matter (copyright page, dedication, acknowledgements, author notes etc.) is very important – many authors and publishers are starting to put most if not all of this, including the copyright page, at the end of e-books, as most e-readers automatically direct the reader to the table of contents or first chapter on opening the book, and in the traditional position the copyright details would be missed. Also, some sites allow the browsing reader to view the early pages, and if more of your writing is displayed, the more appeal the book will have.

I also recommend putting a call for reviews, "More books by the Author" and "Contact the Author" directly after "The End" and without a page break to encourage people to read more of your work. Reviews are extremely important – the more reviews a book has, the more visible it is to potential readers, especially on Amazon, and a polite request with the link can help.

Take the time to link each of your other books on your "More books by the Author" page to the relevant webpage (and check the links work by pressing "ctrl" when you click on it), whether Amazon or your website for more information and the buy links.

3. Footnotes and Endnotes

Because of the number of types of Kindles and the variety of settings, it is not possible to use footnotes in the normal sense or by using Word's footnote or endnote functions. If your book contains footnotes, the best way of dealing with them is by collating them at the end of the book (although you could also have them at the end of each chapter). Each one will need to be linked individually, in such a way that the reader can click (or touch) the number of the footnote in the text to be taken to the explanation, then click on this to go back to where they were in the book. I have included a footnote here[1] in this section to demonstrate.

First type out your list of footnotes, then once everything is in place it's time to format. In the example of the footnote indicator "1" above, select the figure "1" then click on the downward arrow of the "Styles" box in the "Home" tab, which will give you this screen:

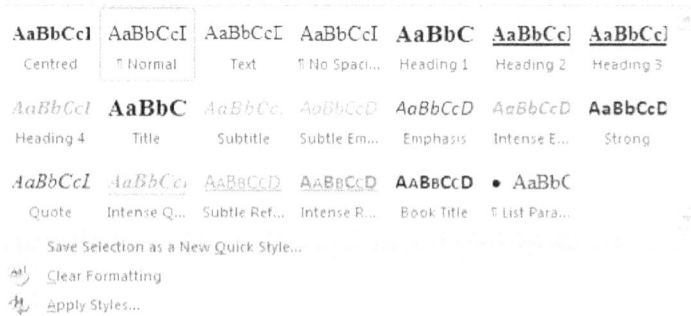

Click on "Save Selection as a New Quick Style".

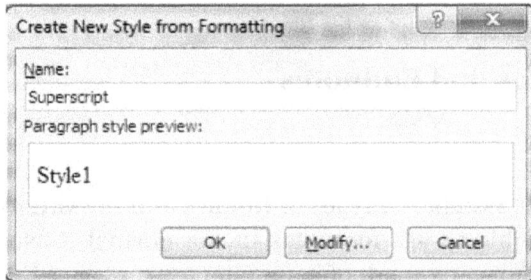

Label your new style as "Superscript" then click on "Modify" to bring up this, by now familiar, dialogue box:

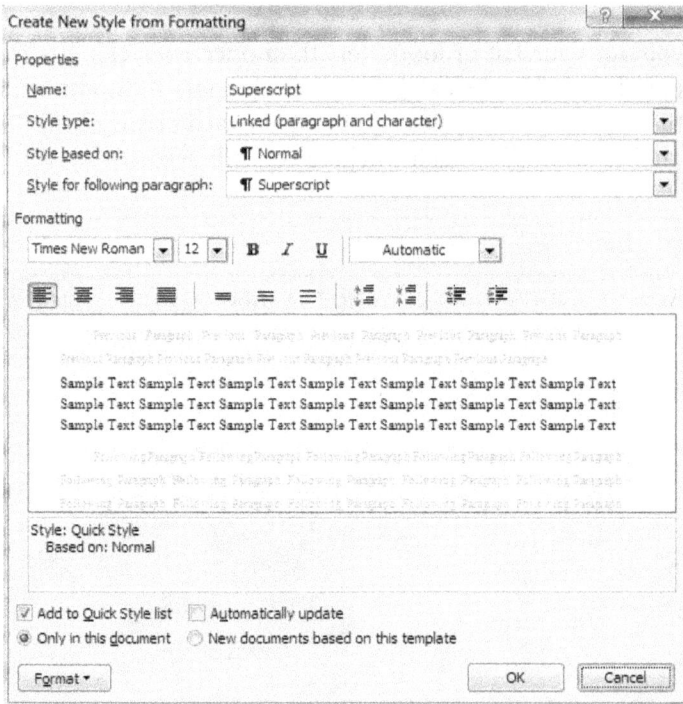

Click on "Format" and "Font".

Tick the box marked "Superscript", then "OK" and "OK" again. Your figure "1" will now be smaller and raised.

Next you need to bookmark both the footnote indicator and the footnote itself in order to link them. Select the footnote indicator "1" and click on "Insert" in the toolbar, then "Bookmark".

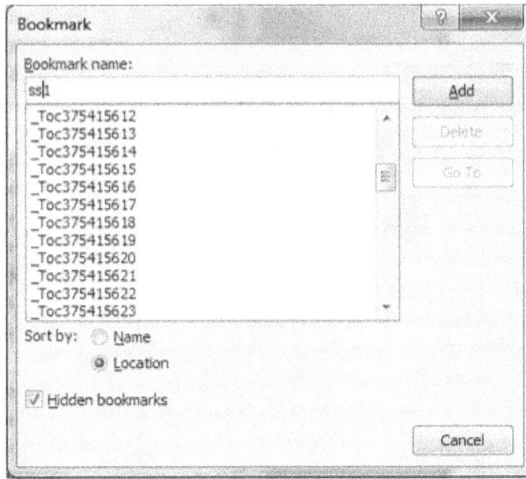

I use the label "ss1" standing for superscript 1, but use whatever will make it easy for you to find and understand. If you are inserting foot/endnotes at the end of each chapter rather than all at the end, then add "c1" etc. to the bookmarks so you can easily distinguish between them. It is not possible to use spaces in the label, so either omit the spaces or use "shift" and "-" to insert the lower dash ("_"). Then click "Add".

Next go to your explanation and select the corresponding number (in this example, "1") and use the same process to bookmark it as "fn1" (footnote 1).

Now that they are bookmarked, it's time to link them. If your footnote number is still highlighted, click on "Hyperlink" in the "Insert" toolbar to bring up this box:

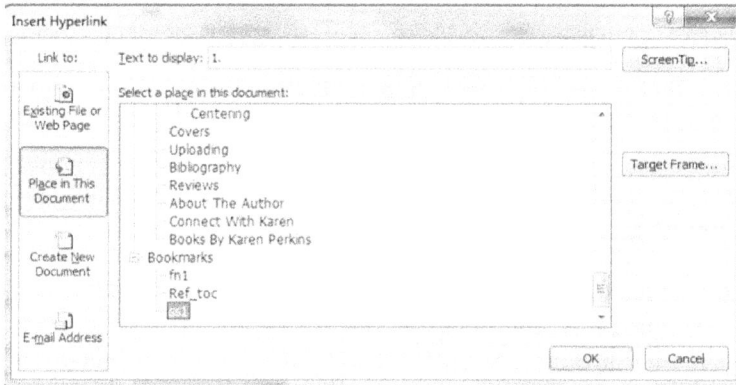

Click on "Place in This Document", then under "Bookmarks" select "ss1" (or however you labelled the footnote indicator in your text), then click "OK". Your footnote number will now come up in blue and be underlined.

Go to the footnote indicator in your text, highlight it and click on "Hyperlink" in the same way, then select "fn1". Your footnote and its indicator are now linked. Clicking on one will take the reader to the other.

1. Clicking on this number on a Kindle will take you back to your place in the text.

4. Pictures

Kindle can handle pictures and picture books as long as the pictures are in JPEG format and less than 127KB in size. To insert a picture, do not cut/copy and paste, but go to the "Insert" tab in the tool bar and click on "Insert Picture". You can then browse your folders to select your picture. Ensure that your picture is centred and not indented to give the best visual impact.

When you have reached the stage of uploading and converting your file (see uploading chapter), do check that the images are not too large. If they are, a red X will show instead of your image, or the image may be incomplete on smaller screens. If your reader is using a larger screen such as a tablet or Kindle Fire, they will be able to enlarge the image(s) if they wish.

If your image(s) are too large, first try to manually reduce their size in your Word file, but if this doesn't work, it/they will need to be compressed. Click on one of your pictures to open the "Picture Tools" toolbar and click on "Compress Pictures":

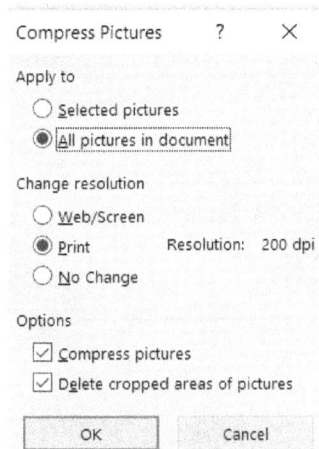

Compress Pictures   ?   ✕

Apply to
○ Selected pictures
◉ All pictures in document

Change resolution
○ Web/Screen
◉ Print   Resolution: 200 dpi
○ No Change

Options
☑ Compress pictures
☑ Delete cropped areas of pictures

OK   Cancel

Untick the box "Apply only to this picture" if appropriate, and choose the resolution option of "Print". Then save your file, reupload to KDP and check the images again in the previewer. If you are still seeing a red X, or if the picture is too large for the smaller screens then go back to "Compress Pictures" and choose "Web/Screen". If that doesn't work, then choose "email resolution" if your version of Word allows it. Click "OK".

But take care: the higher the resolution of the images, the better they will present on a screen, especially if the reader enlarges it, but too low and the reader won't be able to see it at all.

5. Tables

Kindles cannot yet present a table, and I'm afraid you will need to type out your text instead. Please bear in mind that Kindles do not support tabs or columns either, so make it as plain and easy to follow as possible.

6. Em-Dashes

The grammatically correct way to format em-dashes is to use no spaces on either side of the dash. However, in older models of Kindles, this can mean the em-dash connects the words to either side and they are all moved to the next line, disturbing the justification of your text. This does not happen in later models or apps, and is the author's personal choice as to which aspect is of most importance.

7. Symbols

Check each symbol individually on all the options available to you on the Kindle Direct Publishing previewer (see uploading chapter) as different models can handle more symbols than others.

If your symbol is replaced by a small white square on the screen, you will need to change it so that your readers can follow the text.

You have two options: words or an image. If you can replace the symbol with a word, then do so, this will give the most professional layout to your book on a digital device. If, however, you do need the symbol, then you will need to create an image of it, save this as a small JPG and insert it into the file, then check that it is not too large after conversion.

Even if your symbol does convert, spaces may be missing on either side of it. If this happens, go back to your Word source document and add in extra spaces where needed, then retry your conversion.

8. External Links

Use the hyperlink function to add your website, e-mail and social media links to your "Contact the Author" section and the Amazon.com links of your other books to the "More Books by this Author" section.

First select the text you would like to link, then right click and click on "Hyperlink":

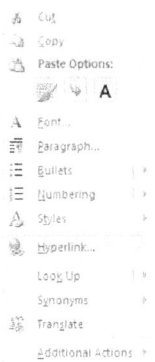

This will bring up the following dialogue box:

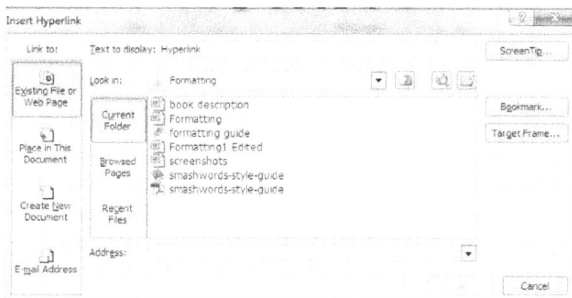

Go to the site or page you want to link and copy the URL by highlighting the web address then pressing "ctrl" and "c".

Go back to your Word document and paste ("ctrl" and "v") the link into the "Address" box and click "OK".

9. White Shading

Always save your Kindle format in the .doc file format (Word 97-2003 File) and avoid .docx, which will help to avoid the problem of white shading in your file. This shading issue is unfortunately invisible in Word itself, as well as on the Kindle previewer function on KDP, but if your reader uses the sepia setting on their Kindle, or prefers white text on a black background, any white shading will be visible and may even make the text unreadable. This is one of the reasons for assigning your entire manuscript to the "Normal" style right at the beginning of the process, and ensuring your font colour is always set to "Automatic".

To check there is no white shading in your file, you will need to do an upload to KDP (see section on uploading) and email the converted .MOBI file to your Kindle.

Change the setting to white on black and scroll through – any white shading will show as white boxes obliterating the text.

If you do find any, go back to your manuscript in Word, highlight the appropriate text and click on the "Clear All Formatting" icon (shown below), then click "Normal" in the styles box, save, re-upload and check again.

Formatting for Epub: Smashwords, Kobo, Nook, iBooks etc.

The formatting for EPUB files is far more complicated than that for Kindle – especially if you are planning to upload to Smashwords. Because Smashwords (and other distribution sites) send books to a large number of retail sites, including Apple, Barnes & Noble and Kobo, their requirements are very stringent, even more so since the introduction of the epubchecker. However, it is still easier to publish through Smashwords than formatting and uploading separately to all the available e-bookstores.

The surest way to ensure your book passes the Smashwords review processes is to use their "Nuclear Method". I'm afraid it is time-consuming, but it is still quicker (and far less frustrating) than taking shortcuts, failing the epubchecker, and trying to work out why and how to fix it.

1. Removing All Existing Formatting

The first step is to remove all existing formatting from the file. This deletes any extraneous bookmarks, links and other issues which may cause problems later. Unfortunately, it also removes italics and bolding, and the styles you have assigned, which will have to be put back in.

1. Open your KINDLE file, select your entire manuscript and copy ("ctrl" "a", then "ctrl" "c"). By working from the Kindle file, you do not have to type out your table of contents.

2. Open the Microsoft programme "Notepad" (usually installed as part of Windows) and paste ("ctrl" "v") your manuscript to create a new document, then close down Word completely.

3. Copy the full text in your Notepad file, re-open Word, and paste your text into this new document. Save as a .doc file (Word 97-2003) and call it "Title SMASHWORDS".

2. Re-Italicize

The best way to replace your italics, bolding and underlining is to use two screens: either an e-reader and a computer, or two computers, one as a source with your master file on the screen (you can transfer a Word file to your e-reader by connecting it to your computer and using Windows Explorer to copy the file and paste it into the relevant folder on your e-reader). Then carefully scan through it to spot each instance of italics etc. and italicize the corresponding text on your EPUB file. It's also worth giving it a final read through before completing the formatting and publishing.

3. Setting Styles

Select the full text and assign it to "Normal" – the details are repeated at the end of this section.

If your book is divided into parts, assign these as "Heading 1" and assign your chapter headings as "Heading 2". Do not insert a page break between "Part One" and "Chapter One" as on some settings in some e-readers (e.g. Kobo), this will automatically happen and some readers may end up with blank pages between the part and chapter headings.

Even if your book is not divided into parts, still assign your chapter headings as "Heading 2" for the same reason – some e-readers may have the chapter heading on a page on its own.

Set your title page to the normal style, then increase the font and bold to your preference – but do not use a font size lager than 18 pt or your file will fail the Smashwords review process.

A reminder of setting Normal and Heading styles follows:

i) Setting the Normal Style

The style tools are under the "Home" tab, on the right-hand half of the toolbar:

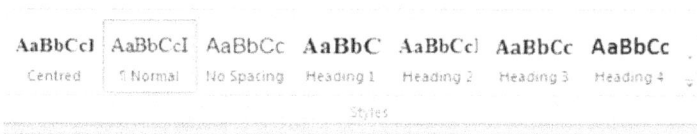

If a style is assigned to your text, its box will be highlighted (in yellow). If nothing is highlighted, select the whole of your document (by pressing "ctrl" and "a"), then right click on the "Normal" style box, which will give you the following options:

Click on "Modify", which brings up the following box:

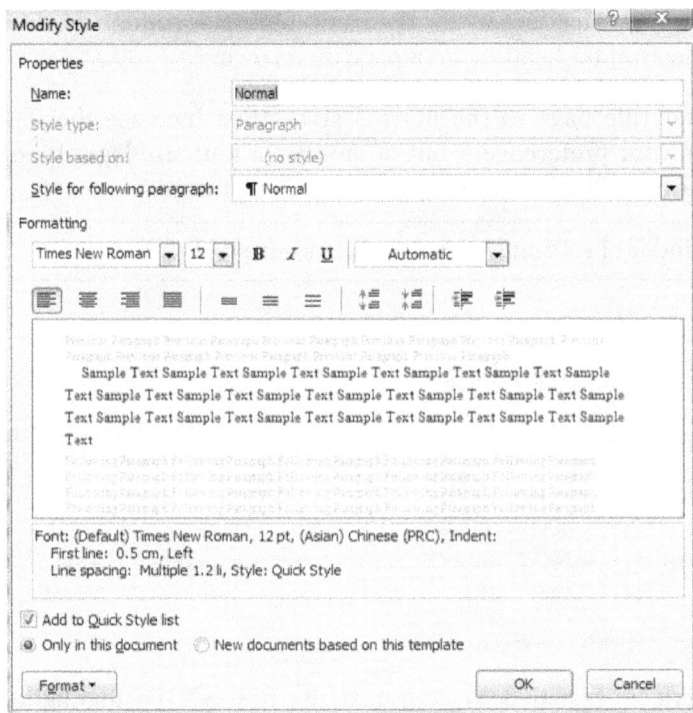

Here you will set the parameters for setting out your manuscript. Because of the number of retailers Smashwords distributes to, it is best to stick to Times New Roman as your font as individual e-readers can then be set to the reader's choice of font. Using other fonts is likely to result in your book failing Smashwords' review process, and may not be licensed for e-books.

Set the font size to 11 or 12 depending on your style of book and personal preference. Then ensure the bold, italics and underlining buttons are not enabled. Click on "Format" at the left-hand bottom corner, and you will have a list of options:

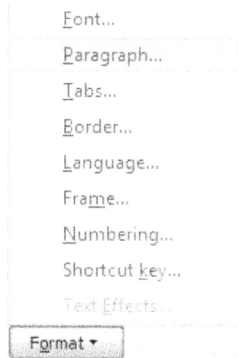

Click on "Paragraph" to bring up the next dialogue box and complete it as follows:

Alignment: Justified
Outline Levels: Body Text
Indentation:
Left: 0 cm
Right: 0 cm
Special: First Line 0.5 cm
Spacing:
Before: 0 pt
After: 0 pt
Line Spacing: Multiple 1.15

Then click "OK", which takes you back to the previous dialogue box. Click "OK" here as well to go back to your manuscript.

ii) Setting the Heading Style

If you have parts to your book, select your first "part" heading and assign the "Heading 1" style by selecting the heading and clicking on "Heading 1". Some e-readers will put the next heading on a new page automatically, so do not put a page break between "Part One" and "Chapter One", and always assign your chapters as "Heading 2" and use the same parameters (even if your book does not contain parts).

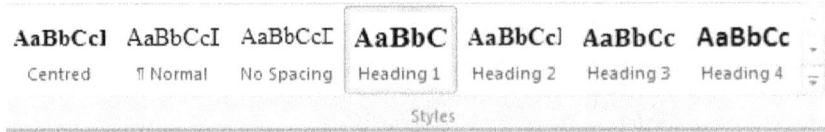

AaBbCcl	AaBbCcI	AaBbCcI	**AaBbC**	AaBbCcl	AaBbCc	AaBbCc
Centred	¶ Normal	No Spacing	Heading 1	Heading 2	Heading 3	Heading 4

Styles

The next stage is to modify "Heading 1" by right-clicking on it as we did before with "Normal".

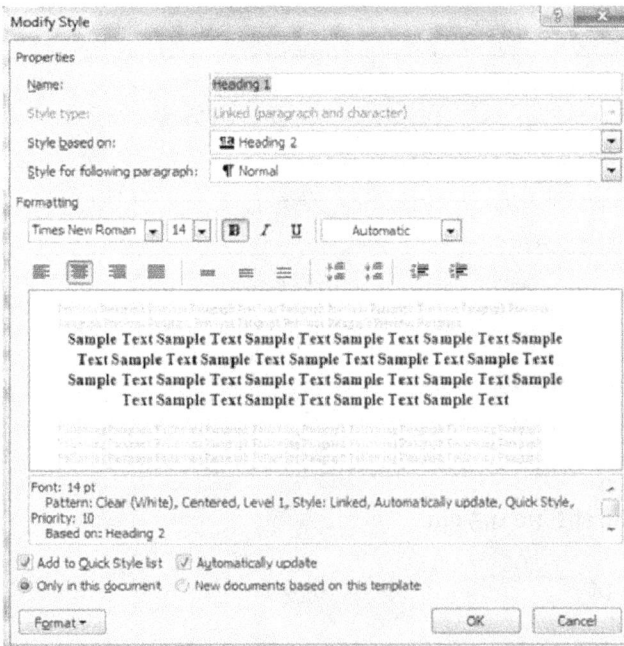

Keep the font as Times New Roman, but here use a larger size. My standard is 14 as this looks best on e-readers. By ticking the "Automatically Update" box near the bottom, if you want to change your heading style, you can do it on one heading in the manuscript and it will carry through to all your other headings (although it is always worth double-checking that this has worked). Next click on "Format" then "Paragraph" as before to bring up the second dialogue box:

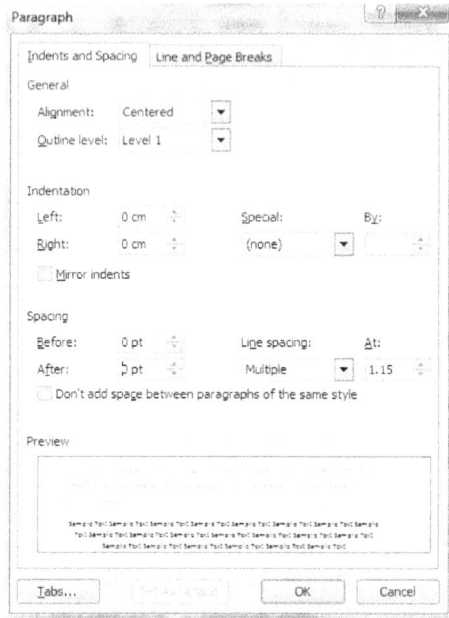

This shows the LionheART standard settings as follows:

Alignment: Centered
Outline Levels: Level 1
Indentation:
Left: 0 cm
Right: 0 cm
Special: None
Spacing:
Before: 0 pt
After: 0 pt
Line Spacing: Multiple 1.15

Click "OK" to close the box and again in the next one.

Select each "part" heading in turn and apply "Heading 1" by clicking on the box, then select each chapter heading and apply "Heading 2". If the navigation pane is not visible, click on "Find" in the top right-hand corner of the toolbar under the "Home" tab, which should bring it up.

Between the chapter heading and the text of the chapter, I recommend inserting two empty lines for presentation, although you can use a single line or none at all if you prefer. Any more than two is too much for the smaller e-readers and can result in empty pages being inserted in the final e-book.

4. Insert Cover Image at Beginning of File

Some of the retailers like the front cover of your book to be inserted at the beginning of the file, and your book will not pass Smashwords' Premium Catalogue if this is missing, which means it will not be distributed to any other site.

Leave the first line blank, then "Insert" "Image" and select your front cover JPG file. Centre this and put a page break below it.

5. Front and End Matter

The placing of the front and end matter (copyright page, dedication, acknowledgements, author notes etc.) is very important – many authors and publishers are starting to put most if not all of this, including the copyright page, at the end of e-books, as most e-readers automatically direct the reader to the table of contents or first chapter on opening the book, and in the traditional position the copyright details would be missed. Also, some sites allow the browsing reader to view the early pages, and if more of your writing is displayed, the more appeal the book will have.

I also recommend putting a call for reviews, "More books by the Author" and "Contact the Author" directly after "The End" and without a page break to encourage people to read more of your work. Reviews are extremely important – the more reviews a book has, the more visible it is to potential readers, especially on Amazon, and a polite request with the link can help.

Take the time to link each of your other books on your "More books by the Author" page to the relevant webpage (and check the links work by pressing "ctrl" when you click on it), whether a retail site or your website for more information and the buy links.

6. Copyright Page

Your Smashwords copyright page will need a section for an ISBN number (so your book can be distributed to Apple etc.) and also the words "Smashwords Edition".

Regarding ISBN numbers, you can buy these from Nielsen in the UK, or Bowker in the US. Alternatively, Smashwords can assign you a free ISBN, listing you as the author and Smashwords as the publisher.

To do this, you need to upload your file first, then go to the ISBN Manager from your dashboard and select the option to assign a free ISBN, copy and paste it to the copyright page, then re-upload the revised file.

7. Table of Contents

The table of contents needs to be bookmarked and linked individually, but if you used your already formatted Kindle file as the basis for your Smashwords file, at least you will not need to type out your table of contents.

Select each heading in turn (including front and end papers, parts and chapters) and bookmark them (a reminder of how to do this is included at the end of this section). Bookmark your Contents heading as "toc" (without the quotation/speech marks) and, as it is not possible to assign bookmarks numbers alone you need either to bookmark each part and chapter as "p1", "p2", "c1", "c2" etc. or you could use Roman numerals if you find this easier.

Once all your headings are bookmarked, then go to your table of contents, select each item in turn and insert a hyperlink to the relevant bookmark. Do not link your "Contents" heading; by bookmarking it as "toc" this is all it needs.

Once you have bookmarked and linked all your headings, place your cursor over each item in the table of contents (without clicking). This will show you the link assigned to each item and you can double-check you have linked everything correctly.

i) Bookmarking and Hyperlinking

Select your heading and click on "Insert" in the toolbar, then "Bookmark". For your first bookmark, the dialogue box should be blank. If it isn't, then delete everything that appears in there, with the exception of any footnote bookmarks you have set and your contents bookmark, checking under both "Name" and "Location", with "Hidden bookmarks" enabled.

Type in the name of your bookmark in the "Bookmark name:" box and click "Add". Do this for every heading in your file.

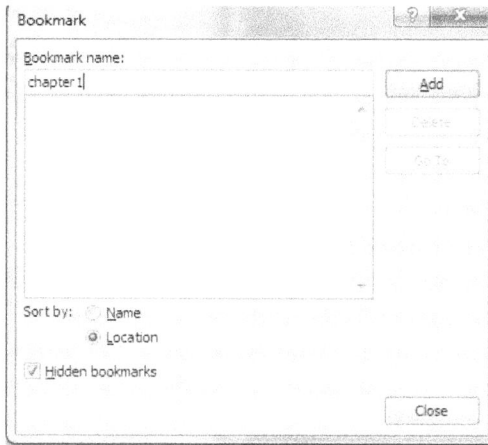

Once you have bookmarked all your headings, it's time to link them. Select the item in your table of contents then click on the "Insert" tab, then "Hyperlink":

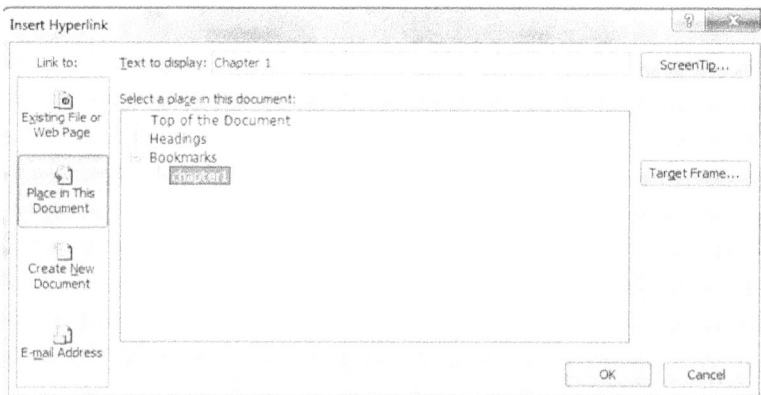

Click on "Place in This Document", then under "Bookmarks" select the appropriate bookmark, then click "OK".

8. Paragraphs

As with the Kindle format, use an asterisk to separate every block paragraph.

If you would like a space between every paragraph, for example in a picture book or reference book, rather than leaving an empty line, format your "Normal" style to include a 10 pt spacing in the "After" box. This will enable your book to pass the Smashwords review and is what I have done in this book.

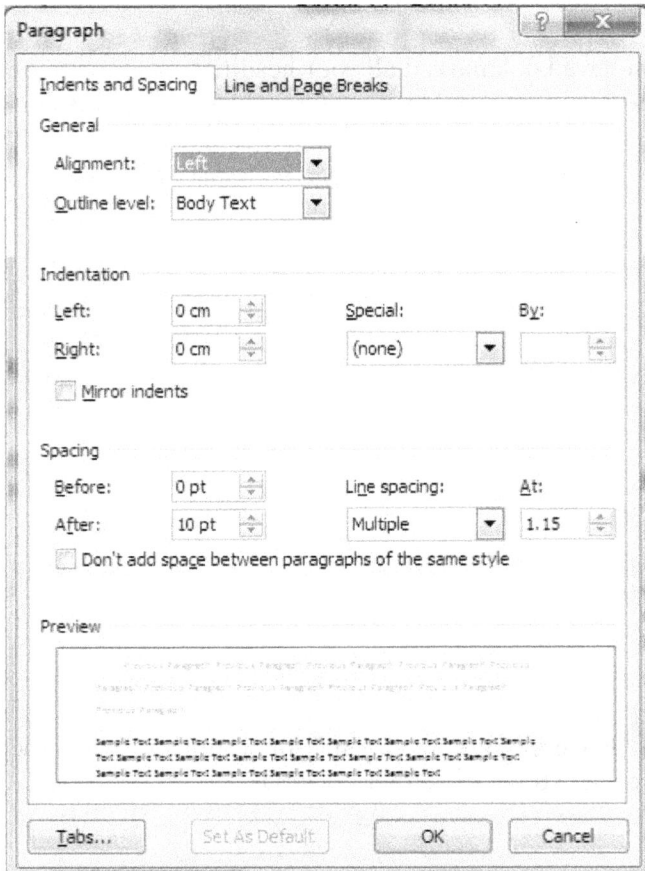

9. Footnotes and Endnotes

Footnotes and endnotes are dealt with in exactly the same way as for Kindle, and this information is repeated below:

Because of the number of types of e-readers and the variety of settings, it is not possible to use footnotes in the normal sense or by using Word's footnote or endnote functions. If your book contains footnotes, the best way of dealing with them is by collating them at the end of the book (although you could also have them at the end of each chapter). Each one will need to be linked individually, in such a way that the reader can click (or touch) the number of the footnote in the text to be taken to the explanation, then click on this to go back to where they were in the book, and I have included a footnote here[1] to demonstrate.

First type out your list of footnotes, then once everything is in place it's time to format. In the example of the footnote indicator "1" above, select the figure 1 then click on the downward arrow of the "Styles" box in the "Home" tab, which will give you this screen:

Click on "Save Selection as a New Quick Style".

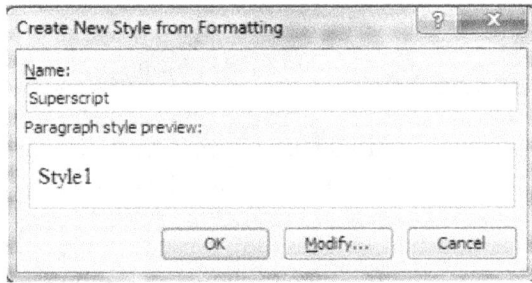

Label your new style as "Superscript" then click on "Modify" to bring up this, by now familiar, dialogue box:

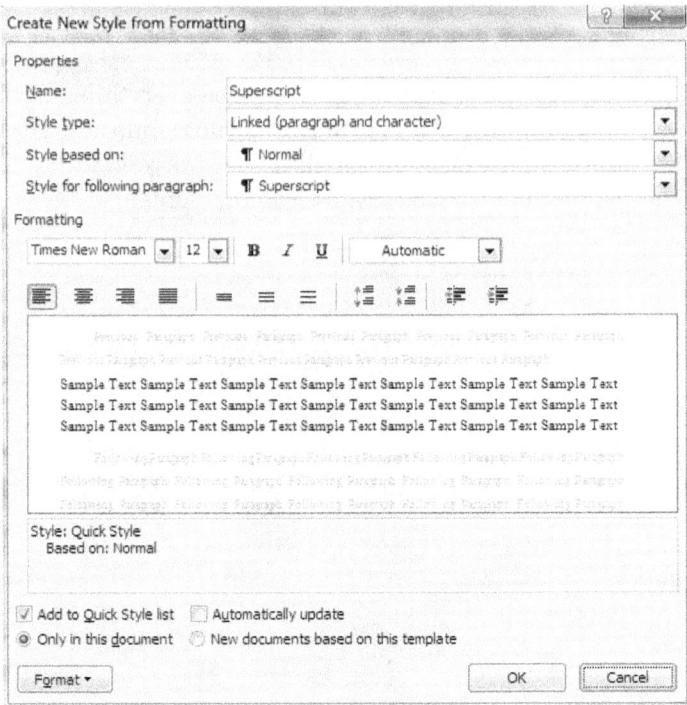

Click on "Format" and "Font".

Tick the box marked "Superscript", then "OK" and "OK" again. Your figure "1" will now be smaller and raised.

Next you need to bookmark both the footnote indicator and the footnote itself in order to link them. Select the footnote indicator "1" and click on "Insert" in the toolbar, then "Bookmark":

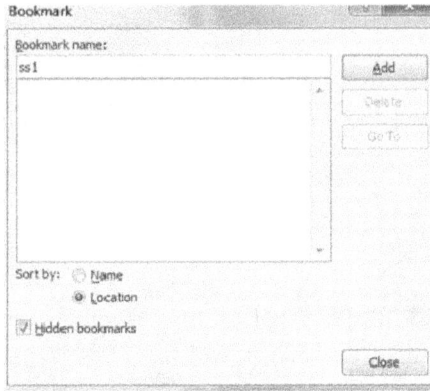

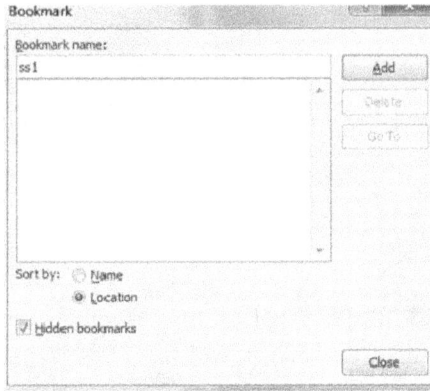

I use the label "ss1" standing for superscript 1, but use whatever will make it easy for you to find and understand. If you are inserting foot/endnotes at the end of each chapter rather than all at the end, then add "c1" etc. to the bookmarks so you can easily distinguish between them. It is not possible to use spaces in the label, so either omit the spaces or use "shift" and "-" to insert the lower dash ("_"). Then click "Add".

Next go to your explanation and select the corresponding number (in this example, "1") and use the same process to bookmark it as "fn1" (footnote 1).

Now that they are bookmarked, it's time to link them. If your footnote number is still highlighted, click on "Hyperlink" in the "Insert" toolbar to bring up this box:

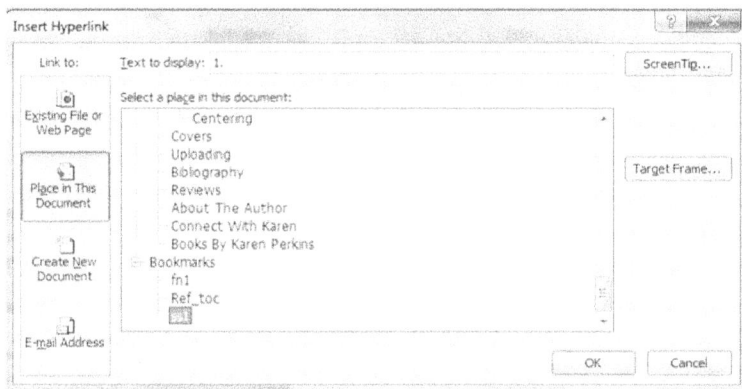

Click on "Place in This Document", then under "Bookmarks" select "ss1" (or however you labelled the footnote indicator in your text), then click "OK". Your footnote number will now come up in blue and be underlined.

Go to the footnote indicator in your text, highlight it and click on "Hyperlink" in the same way, then select "fn1". Your footnote and its indicator are now linked. Clicking on one will take the reader to the other.

1. Clicking on this number on an e-reader will take you back to your place in the text.

10. Fonts

Because of the number of e-readers Smashwords distributes to, it is best to stick to Times New Roman. Individual e-readers can then be set to the reader's choice of font. Using other fonts is likely to result in your book failing Smashwords' review process.

11. Pictures

Images can be included as either JPEGs or PNGs ("Insert" tab on toolbar, then "Picture") and should also be embedded.

To embed your images, click on one of your pictures to open the "Picture Tools" toolbar and click on "Compress Pictures":

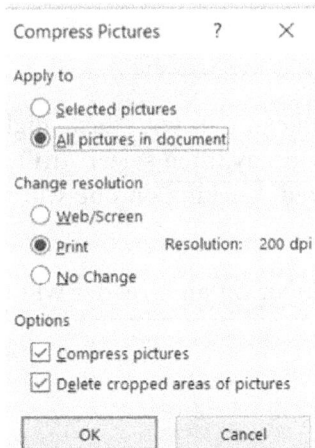

Compress Pictures   ?   ✕

Apply to
  ○ Selected pictures
  ⦿ All pictures in document

Change resolution
  ○ Web/Screen
  ⦿ Print   Resolution: 200 dpi
  ○ No Change

Options
  ☑ Compress pictures
  ☑ Delete cropped areas of pictures

     OK   Cancel

Untick the box "Apply only to this picture" and choose the resolution option of "Print". Then save your file, and have a look at how large it is. The higher the resolution of the images, the better they will present on an e-reader screen, especially if the reader enlarges it. But there is a final file size limit on Smashwords of 10MB, which is easily surpassed if you have images.

If your pictures are detailed or contain text (such as the screenshots in this guide) and will not be legible at a lower resolution, then consider having less of them, but at a high resolution instead, and with cropped areas deleted.

Click on "Compress Pictures", then keep the resolution at "No Change" or "Document Resolution" depending on which version of Word you are using. Ensure the change is applied to all pictures, and tick the box labelled "Delete Cropped areas of Pictures", then "OK".

12. Tables

E-readers cannot yet present a table, and I'm afraid you will need to type out your text instead. Please bear in mind that e-readers do not support tabs or columns either, so make it as plain and easy to follow as possible

13. Symbols

You can insert symbols into your text by using the "Insert" tab, then clicking on "Symbol", but not all of them will convert for e-readers. Check each symbol individually in Adobe Editions (see later chapter) to ensure they present properly.

If your symbol does not appear correctly on the screen, you will need to change it so that your readers can follow the text.

You have two options: words or an image. If you can replace the symbol with a word, then do so, this will give the most professional layout to your book on a digital device. If, however, you do need the symbol, then you will need to create an image of it, save this as a small JPG and insert it into the file, then check that it is not too large after conversion.

Even if your symbol does convert, spaces may be missing on either side of it. If this happens, go back to your Word source document and add in extra spaces where needed, then retry your conversion.

14. External Links

Use the hyperlink function to add your website, e-mail and social media links to your "Contact the Author" section and the Smashwords links of your other books to the "More Books by the Author" section. Do not include any links or references to Amazon or any other online bookstore except Smashwords in your Smashwords file as this will result in your book failing their review process.

First select the text you would like to link, then right click and click on "Hyperlink":

This will bring up the following dialogue box:

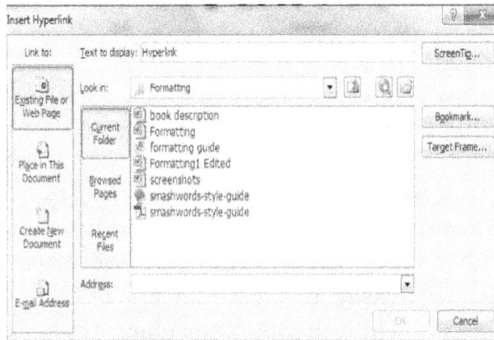

Go to the site or page you want to link and copy the URL by highlighting the web address then pressing "ctrl" and "c".

Go back to your Word document and paste ("ctrl" and "v") the link into the "Address" book and click "OK".

15. Converting to EPUB

There is a choice of software which can convert your Word file to EPUB, and I've found Calibre (http://calibre-ebook.com/) to be relatively simple and quick to use. Upload your Word file (in the .docx file format).

Click "Convert Books", check that Calibre has pulled your cover image through from your file (if not, click on the browse icon under "Change Cover Image" and upload it), add your metadata, then click on "EPUB Output" and select "Preserve Cover Aspect Ratio" to keep the relative dimensions of your cover. Then click on "OK".

When your file has converted, double click on its title to check how it looks in the Calibre viewer. Here you will see if you have any extra pages (sometimes caused by having too many paragraph breaks together), or if your images are too large.

When you are happy with your EPUB, click on "Save to Disc" which will set up a new folder in Explorer including the source files and EPUB.

You can now check your file externally. If you have a Nook or Kobo, you can transfer your file via USB and scroll through it on your e-reader. Set your e-reader to its sepia setting, or white text on black if you have this option, this way you can check if there is any white shading in your file. This shading issue is unfortunately invisible in Word itself, as well as on the Calibre previewer, but if your reader uses either of these settings, any white shading will be visible and may even make the text unreadable.

The first steps of your EPUB format should negate this happening, but if you have made any edits since that stage, especially a cut and paste, white shading may have come with it. If you do find any, highlight the affected area in your Word file and click on the "Clear All Formatting" icon on the Home tab and reapply the Normal style.

There are two other checks that are vital before uploading to Smashwords, or any other retailer: an EPUB validator and Adobe Editions.

16. EPUB Validator

I recommend you check your EPUB by using a validator such as: http://validator.idpf.org/

Click on "Choose File", select your EPUB, then click "Validate". After a few moments you will hopefully be directed to a screen saying *Congratulations! No problems were found in . . .*

If problems are detected, you will be presented with a table with details. This can be a little daunting, but each entry will indicate where in the file the problem occurs and the nature of the problem. Go back to Calibre, right click on your book title and choose "Edit Book" to fix.

A common error picked up here is: *Filename contains spaces, therefore URI escaping is necessary. Consider removing spaces from filename.*

Type	File	Line	Position	Message
WARNING	./tmp/uploads/1468182271112_0000027291/mobiFile/TimesNewRoman.epub/fonts/Times New Roman - Bold.ttf-1 -1)	-	-	Filename contains spaces, therefore URI escaping is necessary. Consider removing spaces from filename.

This means there are spaces in the font file names. To fix it, go back to Calibre and right click on your file name, then click on "Edit File".

Scroll down the list of indices on the left-hand side until you come to "Fonts". Here the file names for the fonts you have used are listed. Right-click on each file name and remove the spaces. Clicking on to the next file name will save your changes.

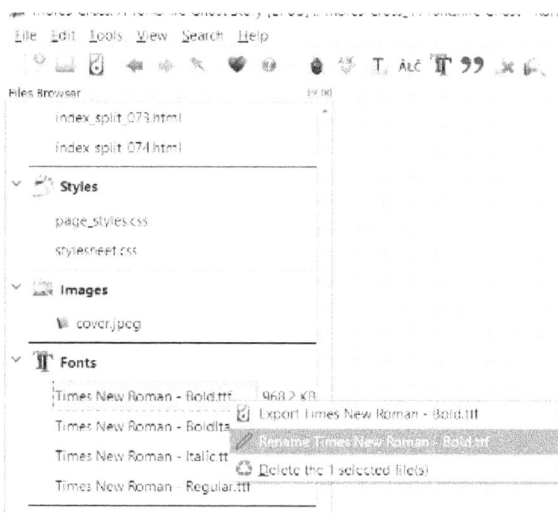

Save your file, close the editor, then save to disc as before and try the EPUB validator again.

Another common error message is: "Fragment identifier is not defined", and this usually means something has not been bookmarked and linked properly. To fix it you will need to go back to Calibre and open the file editor.

The file name given: index_split_002.html refers to the page of the EPUB – double click on this entry in the list on the left-hand side of the editor to open the page:

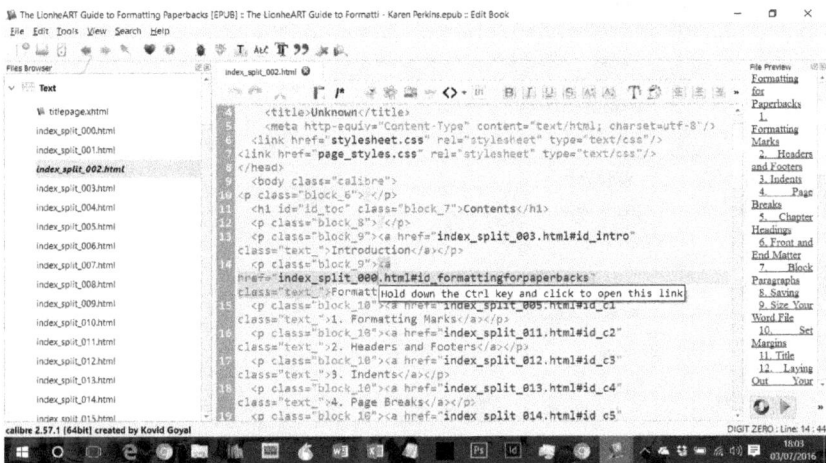

The error message also gave you the line where the problem lies:14. In this case the index split 002 is the table of contents, and line 14 refers to the entry "Formatting for Paperbacks". Go back to your Word document, and redo the bookmark on this chapter heading, then relink in the table of contents. Save your work, reupload to Calibre to convert, then run it through the EPUB validator again. Hopefully you will see this message:

If you are unable to find the cause of the error message, e.g: "Could not parse", then removing all existing formatting as detailed in the beginning of this section should deal with most issues. If you have already done this, then I would do a test conversion after each stage and run it through the validator. If it comes up with an issue, that way you will know where the problem lies.

17. Adobe Editions

Once your file has passed the EPUB validator, it is then time to check it in Adobe Editions. If you don't have this free software, you can download it from: http://www.adobe.com/uk/products/digital-editions/download.html

Upload your EPUB by clicking on "File", then "Add to Library", then you can browse for your file in Windows Explorer and double click on it to load it to Editions.

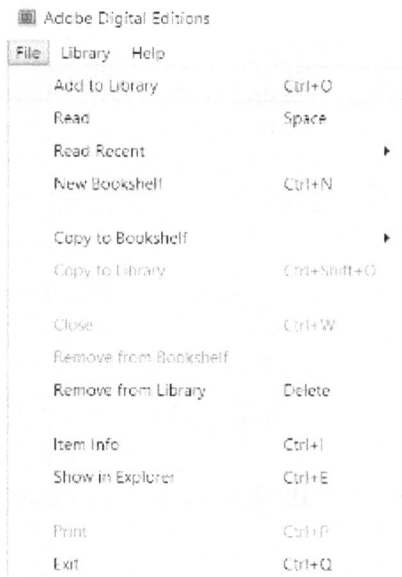

Once your file is loaded to your library, double click on it to open the book, then click on "Table of Contents" on the left-hand side to show the contents panel.

Go through every entry on the contents panel, making sure you click on every arrow to show all your subheadings, if appropriate.

Adobe Digital Editions - The Valkyrie Series: The Fi

File   Edit   Reading   Help

◀ Library   🔖   ☰

🗏 Table of Contents   🗏 Bookmarks

⚙.

Chapter 1

(Untitled)

Chapter 2

Chapter 3

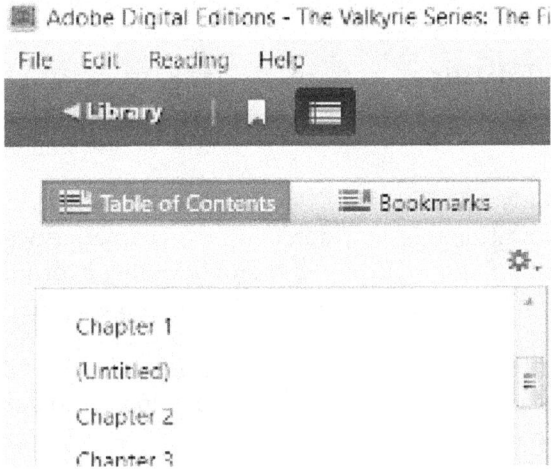

If the word *Untitled* appears anywhere, make a note of which chapter it comes under, then go to that chapter in your source Word file. It is most likely that a page break or empty line has been assigned one of the heading styles. Place your cursor on the page break or empty line and assign it to "Normal".

Once you have cleared every instance of this, delete the book from Editions by clicking on "Library", selecting the book, then click on "File" and "Remove from Library". Next, reconvert your Word file to EPUB through Calibre, and recheck it through the validator and Adobe Editions.

Once you have passed all these checks, you are then ready to upload your EPUB to publish.

Paperback Formatting

The paperback formatting is very different than that for e-readers. For paperbacks, what you see in Word *is* what you get in the end book, and most of the fonts available in Word are also licensed for print so you can add your own personal style to your books.

1. Size Your Word File

The first step is to size your document to that of your finished book. I have found the most popular sizes to be 6 x 9" or the trade paperback size 5.06 x 7.81" but there are also many more options for you to choose from.

Taking 6 x 9" as an example, click on the "Page Layout" tab on your toolbar, click on "Size", then "More Paper Sizes" which will give you this dialogue box:

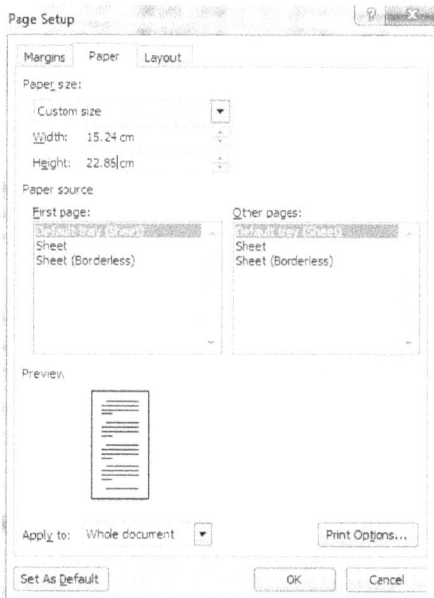

The size needs to be set in centimetres, and for 6 x 9" this converts to a width of 15.24 cm and a height of 22.86 cm. Make sure the "Apply to" box shows as "Whole Document", then click "OK". Your page size will now be set.

For 5.5" x 8.5" books, the width is 13.97 cm and height 21.59 cm.

For 5 x 8" books, the width is 12.7 cm and height 20.32 cm.

For 5.06 x 7.81" books, the width is 12.852 cm and height 19.837 cm. (If using one of these last two sizes I also recommend adjusting your indent to 0.3 cm by adjusting the "Normal" style, which results in a more balanced look to the page).

If you would like a different size, the easiest way to find the correct measurements is to log on to CreateSpace, click on "Add New Title", complete the information on the first screen with your title, select "paperback" and choose the "Guided" option. The next screen asks for more information about your book; you will need to enter an author name and language at this stage before clicking "Save and Continue" to move on, but the remainder of the information can be completed later. Click "Next" on the next screen which is asking you to choose an ISBN option (I will cover the upload process in detail later in the book). You should now have this screen:

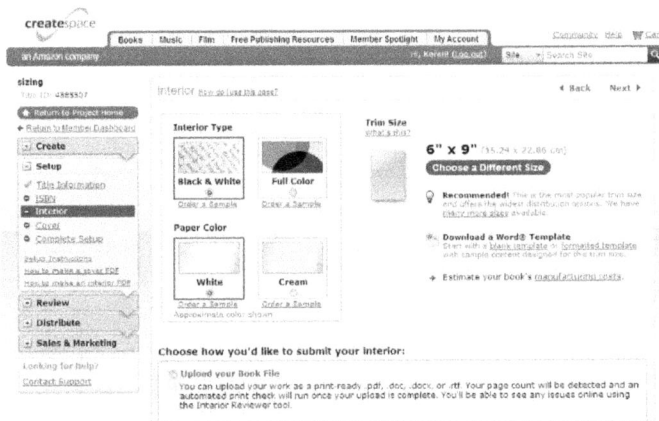

Click on "Choose a Different Size" then select the appropriate option. This will take you back to this screen, and should show your selected size at the top in both inches and centimetres.

2. Set Margins

Again I will use the example of a 6 x 9" sized book. With your file open, click on "Page Layout", "Margins" and choose "Custom Margins".

For a 6 x 9" book, the values to enter are:

Top: 1.9 cm
Bottom: 1.9 cm
Left: 1.9 cm
Right: 1.9 cm
Gutter: 0.63 cm
Gutter position: Left

Again make sure this applies to the whole document, then click "OK".

For 5.06 x 7.81" books, I use top, bottom, left and right values of 1.6 cm, and set the gutter to 0.5 cm.

These are the minimum values to use, you are free to set larger margins if you wish to create a smaller area of text on the page of the finished book.

If your book has more than 400 pages, you will need to set a larger gutter to accommodate the wider spine – minimum 0.875 cm for 6 x 9" books or 0.63 cm for 5.06 x 7.81", and books with over 700 pages need a gutter of at least 2.22cm, and it is worth checking the requirements of the site/printer you are using before going any further with the format. I would also do a dummy upload at this stage if using an unusual margin and run the book through CreateSpace's previewer to check there are no issues before continuing (see uploading section for details of how to do this).

3. Title

Next is the styling of the title on the very first page of your book. You are free to be as artistic as you like here, using your own selection of font and whichever size you would like, although do pay attention to the balance of the words on the page.

4. Laying Out Your Front Papers

The placing of the front and end matter (copyright page, dedication, acknowledgements, author notes, etc.) is very important.

Whilst the title page is always the first page, the copyright page is always second (the only exception is if you insert a page(s) of reviews of your work).

Apart from asserting copyright, you also need to add your ISBN to this page. You can buy these from Nielsen in the UK, or Bowker in the US. Alternatively, CreateSpace can assign you a free ISBN, listing you as the author and CreateSpace as the publisher. To find this number, start the upload process (see later section) and click on "Free CreateSpace Assigned ISBN". Copy and paste this number into your copyright page, then ensure the font and centring matches the rest of the page.

The copyright page is always centred in print books, and the easiest way to do this without affecting the rest of your manuscript is to create a "Centred" style and assign it to this page.

To create a Centred style, select your copyright information then click on the downward arrow of the "Styles" box in the "Home" Tab, which will give you this screen:

AaBbCcl	AaBbCcl	AaBbCcI	AaBbCcI	**AaBbC**	AaBbCcl	AaBbCcl
Centred	¶ Normal	Text	¶ No Spaci...	Heading 1	Heading 2	Heading 3
AaBbCcl	**AaBbC**	*AaBbCc.*	*AaBbCcD*	*AaBbCcD*	*AaBbCcD*	**AaBbCcD**
Heading 4	Title	Subtitle	Subtle Em...	Emphasis	Intense E...	Strong
AaBbCcl	*AaBbCc,*	AABBCCD	AABBCCD	**AABBCCD**	• AaBbC	
Quote	Intense Q...	Subtle Ref...	Intense R...	Book Title	¶ List Para...	

Save Selection as a New Quick Style...

Clear Formatting

Apply Styles...

Click on "Save Selection as a New Quick Style".

Create New Style from Formatting

Name:

Centred

Paragraph style preview:

Style1

OK   Modify...   Cancel

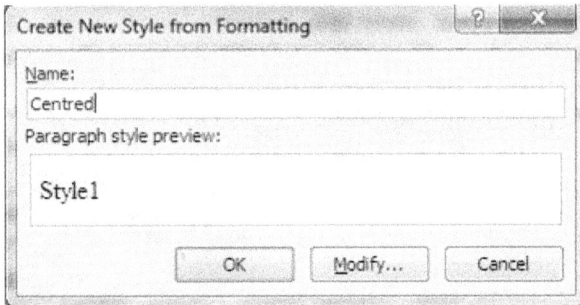

Label your new style as "Centred" then click on "Modify" to bring up this, by now familiar, dialogue box:

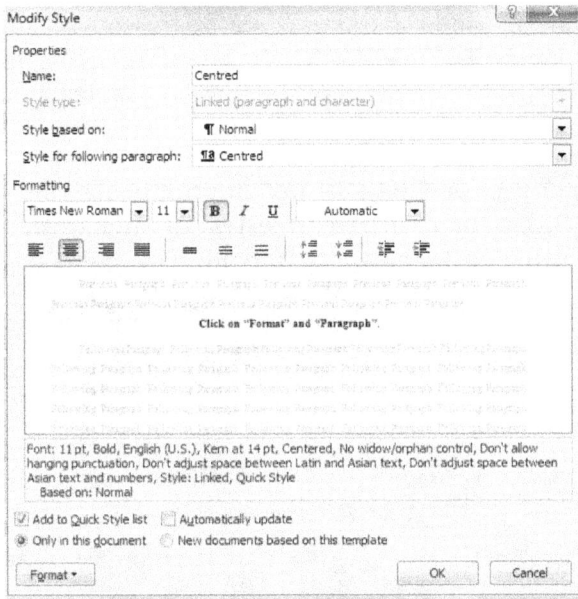

Modify Style

Properties

Name: Centred

Style type: Linked (paragraph and character)

Style based on: ¶ Normal

Style for following paragraph: ¶a Centred

Formatting

Times New Roman ▼ 11 ▼ **B** *I* U̲   Automatic ▼

Click on "Format" and "Paragraph".

Font: 11 pt, Bold, English (U.S.), Kern at 14 pt, Centered, No widow/orphan control, Don't allow
hanging punctuation, Don't adjust space between Latin and Asian text, Don't adjust space between
Asian text and numbers, Style: Linked, Quick Style
Based on: Normal

☑ Add to Quick Style list   ☐ Automatically update
◉ Only in this document   ○ New documents based on this template

Format ▼   OK   Cancel

Click on the "Centre" button, and also set your font size – it is completely up to you whether you have the font the same size as the rest of your manuscript or slightly smaller here. Then click on "Format" and "Paragraph".

The main thing here is to ensure there are no indents or spacing set. Click "OK" then "OK" the next screen and your copyright page should now be centred.

Now set out the remainder of your front papers, for example any author notes and your dedication. If you have a number of front papers, it is then a good idea to have a page containing only the title immediately before your first chapter or prologue.

Keep an eye on the page number (bottom left of your screen on Word) as odd pages correspond to the right-hand (recto) pages of your book, and even pages correspond to the left-hand (verso) pages of your book. Dedications and title pages should always be on an odd page, and your first chapter should also always start on a right-hand page. Insert blank pages if need be using the "Page Break" function to arrange the pages left and right as appropriate.

I recommend putting a call for reviews, "More books by the Author" and "Contact the Author" directly after "The End" to encourage people to read more of your work. Reviews are extremely important – the more reviews a book has, the more visible it is to potential readers, and a polite request can help.

5. Table of Contents

If your book has a table of contents, this is inserted directly before your foreword, introduction, prologue or first chapter as appropriate. Whilst the method is very similar to that explained earlier, there is one difference: page numbers.

I always insert it at this stage so that I know how many pages it will take up and how the page layout in the rest of the book is affected. However, some of the next steps will affect the page numbering, so always update the table as the final formatting step.

First of all type out your heading: "Contents" or "Table of Contents" and assign it to "Heading 1".

Insert empty lines before and after the heading to match the way you have presented the start of your chapters, then click on the next line to place your table of contents.

Click on the "References" tab on your toolbar, then "Table of Contents" at the left-hand side, then click on "Insert Table of Contents" near the bottom of the dialogue box. By doing this rather than using one of the automatic tables you have the option to modify and style your table to your own preferences.

In the next dialogue box, below, click on "Modify":

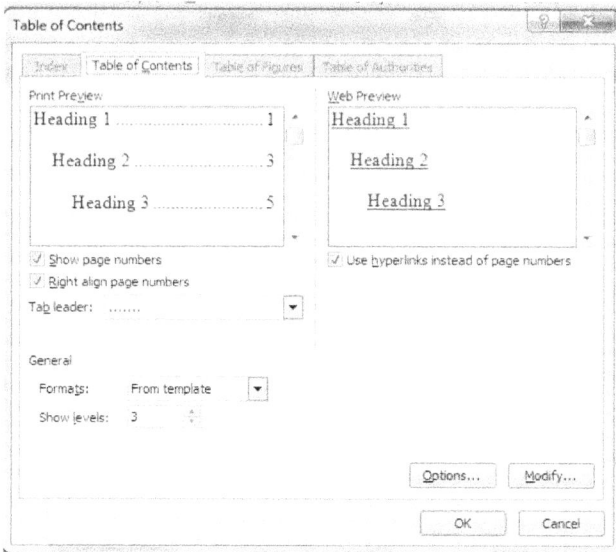

Then on "Modify" again in the next box.

The next box should be familiar to you as it is the same as you used when you modified the Normal and Heading 1 styles.

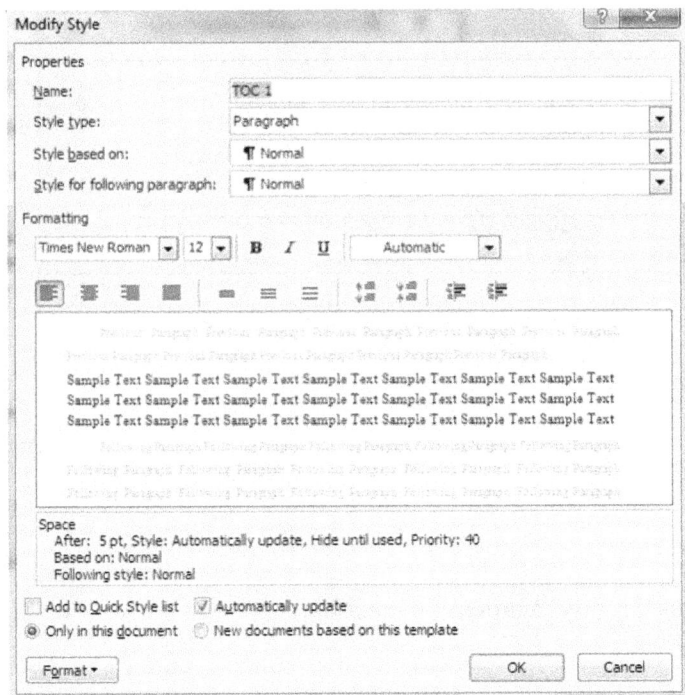

This is where you can put your own style on your table of contents by selecting the font, size and justification of the table. Next click on "Format", then "Paragraph" as before, set the "Special Indent" to "None" and set the spacing according to your own preference.

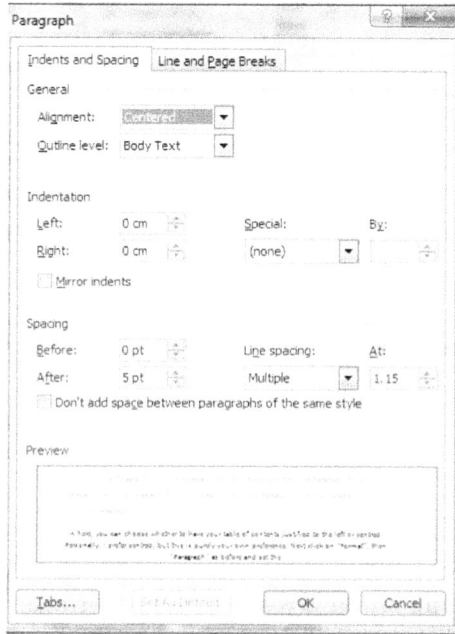

For complicated tables it can be helpful to have a 5 pt spacing as it is easier to read, but if the table is very long, this will add to the number of pages it takes up. You can always change these settings later and try different things until you are happy with your layout.

Next click "OK" to close this box, then the next and the next until you are back at the following screen.

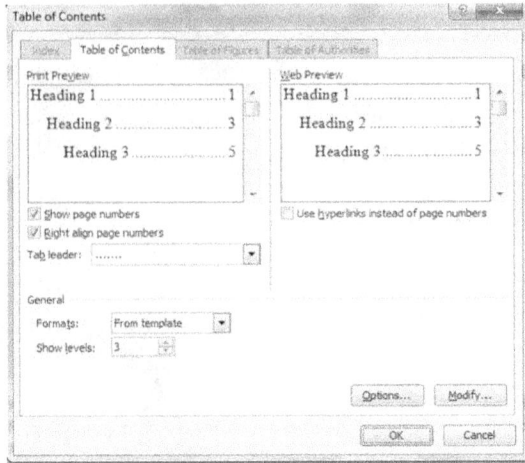

Tick the boxes for "Show page numbers" and "Right align page numbers", and untick the box for using hyperlinks instead of page numbers, then click "OK" (if you have centred your table of contents, you will not be able to right align the page numbers). Your table of contents should now be in place.

Again there will be an entry within the table labelled "Contents" which needs to be deleted. Highlight the entry, taking care that it is only this line that is selected, then press backspace. The table is very sensitive, and if you delete more than you meant to, press "ctrl" and "Z" to undo, and try again.

Don't forget to update the page numbers in your table of contents at the end of the format. To do this, click on "References", then "Update Table", then "Update Page Numbers Only".

6. Headers – Title and Author Name

In most paperbacks, you will see the title of the book and the author name at the top of each page in the main body of the book – but not in the front pages. To set your headers in this way, you need to divide your book into two sections. This is done by replacing your last page break before your prologue or first chapter with a section break.

i) Inserting a Section Break

Click on "Page Layout" in your toolbar, then click on "Breaks":

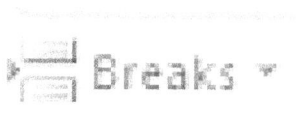

You will then be presented with a list of options:

Click on "Next Page" under the "Section Breaks" heading. You will then most likely have a page break and section break together:

Place your cursor at the join between the two and press enter, then use the left arrow key to place the cursor before the paragraph break and back space to delete it.

----Page Break------------------------¶--------------------------------------Section Break (Next Page)------

You will be left with the section break in place:

¶--------------------------Section Break (Next Page)---

The next step is to insert the headers themselves. At the start of Chapter 1, point your cursor at the top of the page and right click. This will give you an option to "Edit Header". Click on this and the "Header and Footer" toolbar will open:

Tick the "Different Odd & Even Pages" box, and ensure that "Link to Previous" is not highlighted. Then scroll down to the top of your next page – the "Link to Previous" box will again be highlighted. Click on it to unlink to the previous section, then do the same for the footers of each page.

Go back to the header on your Chapter 1 page, and type in the title of your book. Then select this and set the font and size – I usually make the font a little smaller, put into italics, and also put a paragraph break after the title to separate the header from the text. Centre your header and remove the indent by using the slider at the top of your screen in Word.

Click on the upper pointer and move it to the zero position.

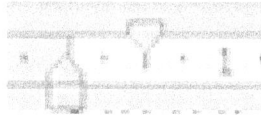

If this is not visible, click on the small symbol at the far right-hand side of your screen, above the scrolling bar which will bring the rulers into view.

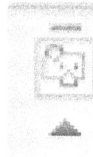

Next do the same thing on the next page, typing in your author name as the header. Now all the right-hand side pages from your first chapter will have your book title at the top, and the left-hand pages your name. Of course, you can have them the other way round if you wish.

To style your book by omitting the header on the first page of each chapter, you will need to make each chapter a separate section by replacing the page breaks with section breaks as above. Select the "Different First Page" option on the Header & Footer toolbar in each section, then delete the header from the appropriate pages.

7. Page Numbers

Similarly to the headers, page numbers start at number one at your prologue or first chapter. While your "Headers and Footers" toolbar is open (or right click on the header as before to open it), "Different Odd and Even Pages" should already be ticked. Unselect "Link to Previous" on both odd and even pages if you haven't already, then click on "Page Number", then "Format Page Numbers".

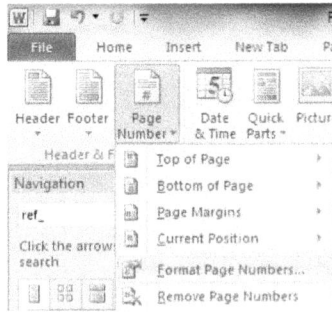

You will now have this dialogue box:

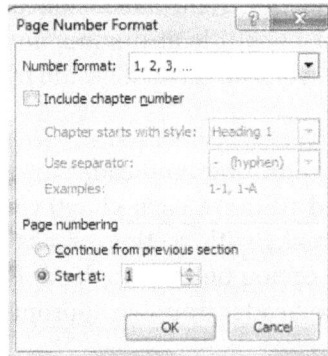

In the "Page numbering" options, select "Start at" and enter "1", then click "OK". Now when we move on to inserting the page numbers, the first page after your section break will be number one.

Click on the footer of your first chapter page, where your first page number will be inserted, click on "Page Number" again, then hold your cursor over "Bottom of page" and you will have three options:

You have the choice of either centring all your page numbers or inserting them at the right-hand corner of your right-hand pages, and left-hand corner of your left-hand pages.

To centre them all, click on "Plain Number 2" in the above box, and do this for both recto and verso pages.

To place your page numbers at opposing sides of your pages, the "Different Odd and Even Pages" box needs to be ticked, then choose "Plain Number 1" for your left-hand (even) numbers, then "Plain Number 3" for your right-hand (odd) numbers.

Then go back to your even numbers, highlight the page number and remove the indent. I also recommend reducing the font size of the page numbers and inserting a paragraph break before the page numbers (on both odd and even pages) to separate them from the text.

When you are done, scroll back to the beginning and ensure no headers or page numbers are on any of the front matter. If there is, go back to the header and footer toolbar at the start of your first chapter, and check that "Link to Previous" is not enabled. If it is, disable it, then scroll up and delete any header or page number from the front pages.

8. Formatting Parts

If your book is split into parts, ensure each part starts on an odd page, and it can also be effective to move the text down to the middle of the page using the enter key to insert paragraph breaks.

9. Formatting Chapter Headings

The style of your chapter headings is dependent purely on your own preferences, and there are a number of things you can do to add interest:

1. Use a stylized font (if it is licensed for general use in print) and a larger font size, in bold.

2. Create a gap above and below the chapter headings. The easiest way to do this is to modify the "Heading 1" style, and add spacings in the "Before" and "After" sections in the "Paragraph" dialogue box. This prevents you from having to make the same changes to each heading individually, e.g:

3. Using an icon, which you would insert as a JPEG picture.

10. Formatting the Start of Each Chapter

i) Dropped Capitals

A nice and professional touch is to start each chapter with a dropped capital as demonstrated here. Firstly, select the letter to be dropped, then go to the "Insert" tab on your toolbar and click on "Drop Cap" then "Drop Cap Options".

In the next dialogue box, click on "Dropped" then set the parameters: font, number of lines and distance from text.

Click on "OK". This will need to be done individually for each chapter.

ii) Capitalisation

ANOTHER OPTION IS to capitalize the first three words (for example) of each chapter as shown here. Select the words to capitalize, then click on the "Aa" symbol and "UPPERCASE". I also recommend you reduce the font size of the capitalized words. At the start of this paragraph, the capitalized words are 2 pts smaller than the rest of the text.

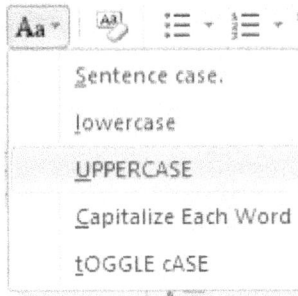

11. Justify Main Text

At present, the main text of your book will still be left justified and it is now time to justify it properly by modifying the "Normal" style.

Right click on "Normal" in the style box on your "Home" tab, click and "Modify":

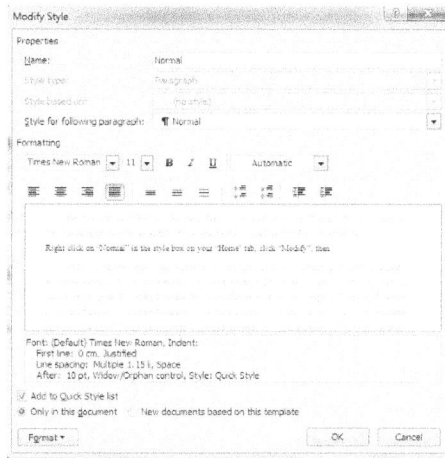

Click on the justification button:

This will justify all the text in your chapters.

12. Laying Out Your End Papers

At the end of the book include a call for reviews, any author note or acknowledgements, social media contacts and the book descriptions of your other titles. Again pay attention to whether they fall on the left- or right-hand page and insert blank pages if need be to set them out as you desire.

13. Page Breaks

Scroll through your book to check for any blank pages within the body of the text. If you do have an inadvertent blank page it will be due to the previous chapter finishing on the very last line of the page and the page break appearing on the next page.

If this has occurred, delete the page break.

Do not have a page break on the same line as any text as this will affect its justification.

14. Footnotes and Endnotes

If your book includes footnotes (explanations placed at the bottom of each page) or endnotes (explanations or further information placed at the end of each chapter or the end of the book) you can use the Word function to place them.

Under the "References" tab on your toolbar, you have the option to "Insert Footnote" or "Insert Endnote". By placing your cursor at the point in the text where you would like the footnote indicator and clicking "Insert Footnote" or "Insert Endnote" as appropriate, Word will place the number (in superscript) and take you to the footnote or endnote itself ready for you to type it in.

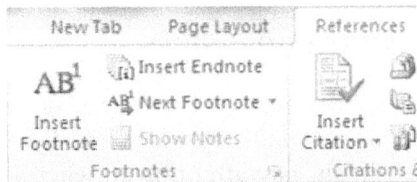

15. Indexing

The indexing function in Word makes indexing your book virtually painless. Go to the "References" tab, then scroll through your book, selecting each word you would like to appear in the index in turn. Click on "Mark Entry" then move to the next indexed word.

Once you have marked every entry, go to the end of the book where you would like to place your index and click on "Insert Index".

16. Embedding Fonts

If you have used any font other than Times New Roman, it will need to be embedded in the file.

To do this, go to the "File" tab, select "Options", then "Save" to bring up this screen:

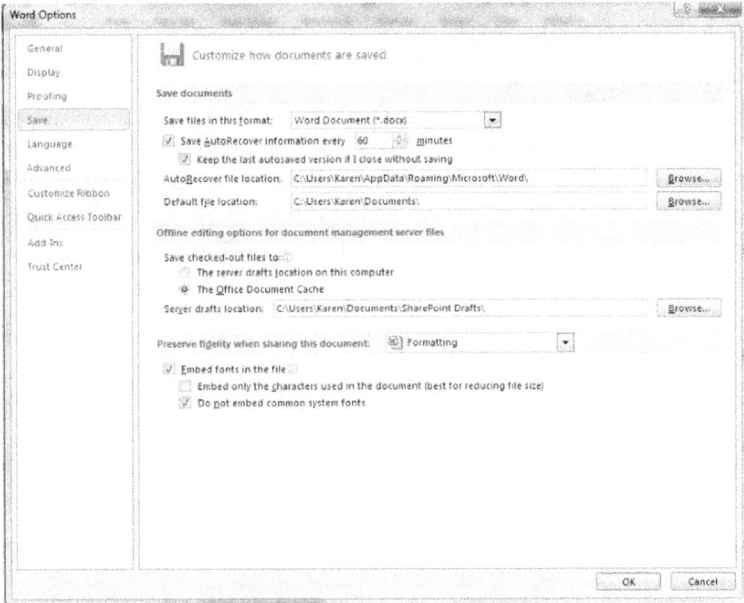

Tick the box marked "Embed Fonts in this file", then click on "OK".

17. Formatting Pictures

Formatting any pictures in your print book is a case of centring each (by assigning your "Centred" Style) and expanding them so they fit within the margins shown in your ruler at the top of your screen in Word, just below the toolbar.

18. Links

If there are any links in your file, highlight each in turn, right click and "Remove Hyperlink". This will change the font colour back to black and remove the underline making them easier to read in print.

19. Check Punctuation Doesn't Cross a Line

This means scrolling through your entire formatted book, paying attention to the start of each line along the left-hand margin. If an ellipsis has been split by a line, or an em dash and closing quotation/speech mark have been split, you will need to adjust the text accordingly. You have two options:

i)   Insert line breaks in the appropriate places to manipulate where the end of the line falls. To do this, place your cursor at the beginning of the word preceding the punctuation series and press "shift" and "enter". This will move the text beyond it to the line below without adding any indents.

If you have a line that is shorter than the others due to a long word having been moved to the line below, you can divide the word with a line break and add a hyphen. Take care to divide the word in such a way that it does not interrupt the flow for the reader, such as dividing between syllables. Do double-check to make sure that the first part of the divided word is not misleading on its own and everything still makes sense.

ii)   Condense the font spacing by selecting the paragraph, right clicking and selecting "Font . . ." Then click on "Advanced", change the Spacing setting to "Condensed" and change the value to "0.1". If that isn't enough, try "0.2", then "0.3" etc. until the problem is solved.

20. Block Paragraphs

In print books, block paragraphs are left blank unless they fall at the end or beginning of a page, in which case an asterisk is used to make it clear to your reader that it is a change of scene, point of view, or time has passed.

In the generic formatting section, you inserted asterisks in every block paragraph and it is now time to delete all those which do not fall at the end or beginning of a page. Once you have done this, put an asterisk into the "Search" box in your navigation pane on the left-hand side of your screen and double-check the positioning of each one.

There should be no indent unless the paragraph/chapter starts with dialogue, in which case it is always indented, whether direct dialogue (speech) or indirect (thoughts). To remove the indent, place your cursor at the start of the line, then press backspace.

21. Widows and Orphans

Widows and orphans are stray words at the very start or end of a page, and a professionally produced paperback will avoid these. In the past anything less than a full line was unacceptable, although most publishers now are happy if there is at least half a line at the top of a page.

There are two ways of dealing with these, the simplest being to enable "Widow/Orphan Control" in Word. To do this you need to modify your "Normal" Style – navigate through "Format" and "Paragraph" as before, then click on the "Page and Line Breaks" tab, then simply select the "Widow/Orphan Control" option and save.

The disadvantage of this method is that it can result in uneven pages where the lines don't match up on the left (verso) and right (recto) sides, and if you would like to address this then the widow and orphan control needs to be handled manually.

It is said that a widow "has no future" and a line following a block paragraph at the bottom of a page is easily dealt with by adding an extra paragraph break and including an asterisk.

An orphan "has no past" and is a little more complicated to deal with. It is very important to start at the beginning of the book, and do this stage last. Ensure the Widow/Orphan control as mentioned above has not been enabled, then scroll through each page, and when you come across an orphan, select both it and the full page before it, then right click and select "Paragraph" to change the line spacing. The value you select will depend on the size of your paperback as well as font and other factors, so will need some trial and error, but I start by changing the value of 1.15 to 1.12.

If this has worked, the text will have effectively moved up one line, negating the orphan, and the bottom of both verso and recto pages will line up. If this is not the case, then adjust the value until you have the desired effect.

Now your file is set out, double-check your asterisks and punctuation as per the previous chapters, ensure each chapter starts on a new page, and then update the page numbers in your table of contents by clicking on the "References" tab, then "Update Table".

22. Converting to pdf

You can upload your Word file to CreateSpace and they will convert it for you (if you do this, save it as a .doc file as .docx does not always keep all the formatting if CreateSpace convert it), or you can convert to pdf yourself which gives you greater control over the finished product.

It is not enough to simply "Save As PDF", as you need it to save on the High Quality Print setting. This means downloading Adobe Acrobat, which does cost, but may be worth it if you publish a large number of titles.

To create your pdf, go to the File tab in Word, then click on "Print". Open the dropdown box under "Printer" and select "Adobe PDF", then click on "Printer Properties" below it, and you will be presented with this box of options:

Ensure the "Default Settings" option is set to "High Quality Print", the next box is "None", then "Prompt for Adobe PDF Filename" to make saving easier. In the fourth option box, choose the size of your manuscript, in this case 6x9".

Click on "Print", then you should be prompted to select a place to save the file. Once your file is converted, it should automatically open in Adobe Acrobat.

Once the pdf is ready, go through it to double-check everything is presented as it should be.

Covers

I cannot stress enough how important it is to get the cover for your book right. As independent authors, our biggest challenge is to find readers, and we find most of our readers online.

Your cover not only needs to look fantastic as a paperback, but also needs impact as a thumbnail. If someone is browsing through the online bookstores, they will not click on your book if the cover doesn't make them look twice. On top of that, a poor cover will lead potential readers to expect the writing, editing and formatting to be just as poor and pass your book by – often erroneously – but they'll never find that out unless they read the book.

Once the reader has bought or downloaded your book, your cover still needs to work for you – whether on your reader's bookshelf or on their e-reader (often in black and white).

As authors we want our books to be read – and hopefully reviewed, too – and our covers are instrumental in readers making this decision.

Uploading

Before you upload, carefully consider your author name. As a self-published author, the majority of your book sales will be online, and you want to make it as easy as possible for readers to find you. Initials are difficult and frustrating for people to search for in the online bookstores as spaces and full stops, if added erroneously or missed out in the search box, can result in an empty search on some sites.

In this section, I will take you through the account creation and upload process for the three most commonly used sites for independent authors:

1. Kindle Direct Publishing

2. Smashwords

3. CreateSpace

1. Kindle Direct Publishing

https://kdp.amazon.com/kdp/self-publishing/signin

This site allows you to upload your book direct to Kindle, and gives you the most marketing opportunities and flexibility with categories and presentation on Amazon.

If you already have an Amazon account, you can sign in with the same details, but if not, creating an account is simple. First, select the appropriate sign-in option:

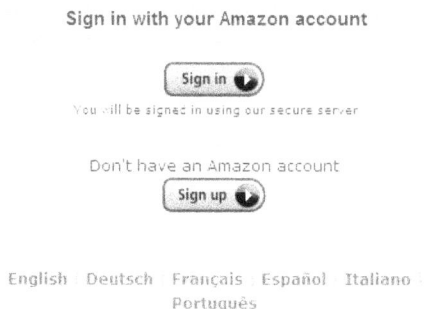

Sign in with your Amazon account

Sign in

You will be signed in using our secure server

Don't have an Amazon account

Sign up

English Deutsch Français Español Italiano
Português

and you will be taken to the sign-in screen:

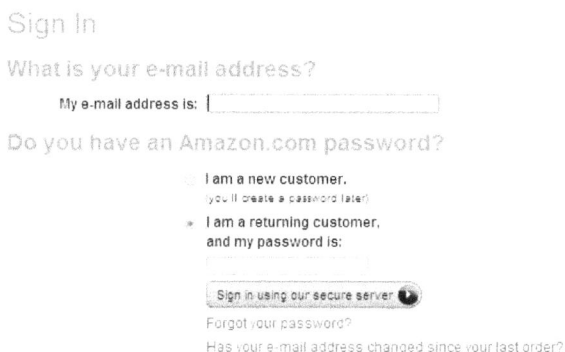

Sign In

What is your e-mail address?

My e-mail address is:

Do you have an Amazon.com password?

I am a new customer.
(you'll create a password later)

I am a returning customer,
and my password is:

Sign in using our secure server

Forgot your password?
Has your e-mail address changed since your last order?

When you have completed your details you will be taken to your bookshelf:

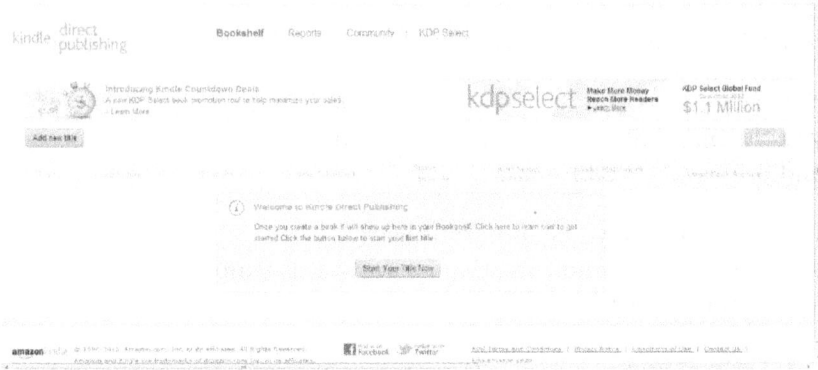

If this is a new account, click on the "(your name) Account" button at the top of the screen, and follow the steps through to complete your personal details, including postal address and telephone number, then "Your Royalty Payments" section.

In here you will need to complete your bank account details, including bank name, branch name, IBAN (International Bank Account Number) and SWIFT/BIC code if you live outside the US. If these are not printed on your bank statements, you can find them by ringing your bank or calling into your branch. You will need to complete these details, including your tax information (see end of section) before pressing that publish button.

Once your account is set up, you can start the upload process. Click on + Kindle eBook and you will be taken to the first of three screens.

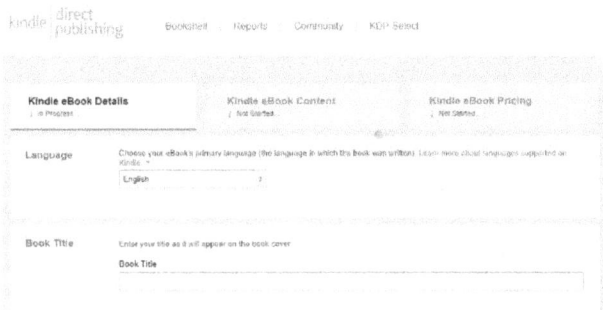

i) Entering Your Book Details

Complete your book title, subtitle and the name of the series, if appropriate, plus the book's number in the series. Subtitles are a useful way of telling browsing readers the genre of your book, as well as reinforcing keywords (more on that later), and it is worth thinking about this carefully, as well as researching books similar to yours to see what works well.

Next, add the edition number, your author name and publisher name if you are using one, then your book description. This description will be used on the Amazon page for your book, and is extremely important. It needs to sell your book to potential readers, so should be professional, punchy, and also grammatically correct with no spelling errors. Any mistakes in here will lead your readers to think your book will be full of typos too.

ii) Verify Your Publishing Rights

If your book is out of copyright or not copyrighted and in the public domain, select this option. Otherwise, if you hold the copyright, click the second option.

iii) Targeting Your Book

In this section you set the categories for your book in the Kindle Store on Amazon. It is worth taking your time to get the right categories (you can assign two) and keywords (seven). Placing your book in the subcategories and themes within main categories can make it much easier to be noticed by browsing readers (especially after running a promotion – see KDP Select below) as well as give you higher positions in search results.

You can find the relevant categories, subcategories and themes on Amazon by clicking on "Departments" below left of the Amazon search bar, selecting Kindle Books, then refining your choices as appropriate for your book, and matching them as closely as possible to the category choices given in the list on KDP.

Once you have chosen which categories and subcategories you would prefer, go back to Amazon to examine any themes listed. These are different for each category, for example, the Romance category has options for romantic hero, plus themes such as beaches, vacation, second chances. Other useful keywords are the time period if your book has any historical elements, and place names.

There is a great deal of scope, and it will likely take some experimentation to place your book in the categories you are hoping for. KDP do have guidelines if you get stuck (available in their help section), and if this still doesn't help, you can contact them direct and they will help you.

There is also a section here for children's and young adult books to set the appropriate age ranges. If you write for adults, just leave this section blank.

iv) Pre-Order

You have the option here to set a release date in the future, which can be useful in helping you plan launch promotions etc. Do ensure your book will be ready a few days ahead of time though, as you will be unable to change your file in the run-up to the release. Amazon will email you to give you the date they will require the final file.

Clicking on "Save and Continue" will take you to the second screen, Kindle eBook Content:

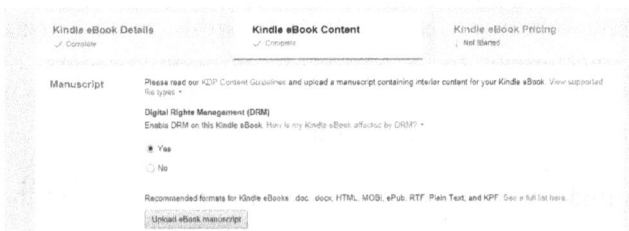

v) Manuscript

Enable Digital Rights Management here – this helps to protect your book against piracy (although unfortunately is not foolproof), then click "Upload eBook Manuscript" and select your "Title KINDLE" file. The site will then take a few minutes to upload your file and convert it to the .MOBI format.

vi) Book Cover

If you have a cover to use, click on "Upload a Cover You Already Have" and select your cover image, which should include your subtitle as well as title and author name. This should be a JPEG or TIFF file, and I have directly quoted KDP's dimension guidelines below:

"Requirements for the size of your cover art have an ideal height/width ratio of 1.6, this means:

• A minimum of 625 pixels on the shortest side and 1000 pixels on the longest side

• For best quality, your image would be 1563 pixels on the shortest side and 2500 pixels on the longest side"

If you don't have a prepared cover, KDP do offer a Cover Creation Tool with a number of designs and images you can customize to your liking.

vii) Previewing

You can preview the final file in two ways before moving on, first by using the online previewer by clicking "Preview on Your Computer" which shows you a mock-up of the Kindle Fire plus a selection of other models, and how your book will look. Once you are happy with this you can "Preview on Your Kindle Device", which will download a .MOBI file for you to transfer to your Kindle or app; but first you will need to authorise your Kindle to accept emails from your specific email address (it won't accept any emails without this to guard against spam).

To find your Kindle's email address from Amazon, go to "Manage Your Kindle" in the dropdown box where it says "Hello ......, Your Account", then go to "your devices" which should show your Kindle and its email address. Then go to "Settings", scroll down to "Personal Documents", and input your email address to authorise your Kindle to accept your emails. Once it's set up, you can then email Kindle books and even Word and pdf documents to read on your Kindle or Kindle app.

Do take the time to scroll through every "page" to check the layout. Check your front papers are well presented, your block paragraphs are formatted correctly and ensure all your chapter headings are centred and consistent. Also check your end papers and all the links.

Also check that your images are sized correctly, your symbols present properly, and there is no white shading – if there any issues, check the relevant chapters in the formatting section for solutions.

viii) ISBN

You can then assign an ISBN (International Standard Book Number), although Kindle assigns their own ASIN number to identify each book and an ISBN is not needed.

When you are happy, click "Save and Continue" which will take you to the final screen:

Kindle eBook Details	Kindle eBook Content	Kindle eBook Pricing
✓ Complete	✓ Complete	⌄ Not Started

KDP Select Enrollment **Maximize My Royalties with KDP Select** (Optional)

With KDP Select, you can reach more readers, earn more money, and maximize your sales potential. Learn more about KDP Select. How Do I Enroll? ▾

☐ Enroll my book in KDP Select

Territories   Select the territories for which you hold distribution rights. Learn more about distribution rights

    ◉ **All territories (worldwide rights)** What are worldwide rights? ▾

    ○ Individual territories What are Individual Territory rights? ▾

Royalty and Pricing   **KDP Pricing Support (Beta)**

See the relationship between price and past sales and author earnings for KDP books like yours.

    [View Service]

ix) KDP Select

The first decision is whether or not to enrol your book in KDP Select and there are both advantages and disadvantages to this option.

The main advantage is that you can utilize Amazon's promotion options if you are enrolled: either offering your book for free for five days in every three-month period, or setting a discount price for a set amount of time in their "Countdown Deals" offer. You will also be enrolled into Amazon's Kindle Unlimited scheme, which is a subscription service allowing readers to borrow your book, and can be a good source of potential income, particularly for larger books, as you are paid dependent on how many pages people read.

You also have the opportunity to run marketing campaigns through Amazon Marketing Services, with ads on other books' listing pages or in search results.

The disadvantage is that your e-book has to be exclusive to Amazon (although you are free to publish in paperback).

x) Rights and Pricing

Firstly you will be asked to confirm which publishing rights you hold: worldwide or individual territories, then set your prices in the relevant currencies.

Next choose your royalty option.

The 35% option is usually only used for books priced at less than £1.99 or $2.99, and the 70% option can only be used for books priced above these thresholds.

You have the option of using the US price to dictate the price in other currencies or to set each individually. Bear in mind when you are setting your UK prices that 20% VAT is included.

KDP also have a pricing support service. This is still in beta, but is a very useful tool. By clicking on "View Service", KDP will give you a guideline of which price point offers the highest author earnings for similar books. You can then choose to use this recommendation or set your own pricing.

xi) Kindle Matchbook

This scheme allows people who have bought your paperback through Amazon to receive the Kindle book at a discount or even free. This can be a useful promotional tool, especially near Christmas, encouraging someone to buy your book as a present for a friend and keeping the Kindle version for themselves.

xii) Kindle Book Lending

This allows people who have bought your Kindle book to lend it to their friends for two weeks.

Finally, click "Publish Your Kindle eBook".

Your book will be available on Amazon within forty eight hours – congratulations!

2. Smashwords

https://www.smashwords.com/

Click on "Join For Free!" at the top of the page and complete the details, then click on "Account".

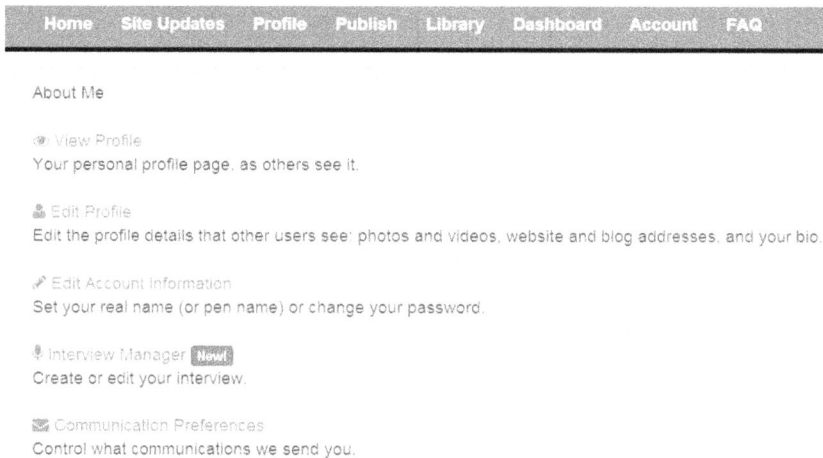

First "Edit Profile" then "Edit Account Information". Smashwords will pay your royalties through PayPal, so you will need enter the e-mail address you use on PayPal in the appropriate box here. You will also need to complete your tax information (see end of section for more details).

Next click on "Publish".

1 Title and synopsis

Title

The title of your book.

Release date

New! Smashwords is beta testing preorders for Apple, Barnes and Noble and Kobo. Learn the benefits of preorders.

• For immediate release (will publish to the Smashwords store in minutes).

○ Make it a preorder — schedule release date in the future. (Visit our preorder help page before you select this option.)

Synopsis

Long description:

The long description of your book appears on your Smashwords book page, and is distributed to most retailers.

Instructions: Your long description will be used to market your book on your Smashwords book page and shared with most retailers. AVOID ALL CAPS and do not enter e-mail addresses, hyperlinks, book prices, or promotions. Limited to 4,000 characters or fewer.

Short description of your book (required):

The short description of your book appears throughout the Smashwords site and is distributed to retailers

0 characters so far, 400 remain

Complete the title, then select whether you would like to release your book immediately, or at a future date (and allow pre-orders if appropriate).

Put your book description into the "Long description" box, and either a concise version or the first paragraph of your description into the "Short description" box.

Next set your language, then price (in US $), followed by your categories by searching through their options – and please do assign two categories to your book to make it easier for browsing readers to find.

The tagging section is very similar to the keywords on Kindle. Choose between one and ten words with which to tag your book to help people find it. All the e-book format options in the next section will be ticked and if you keep it this way Smashwords will convert to all these formats and distribute to all their satellite sites, but bear in mind that some of these formats, e.g. rtf and doc are not secure and the text will be easy to copy. I make my books available as EPUBs and MOBIs only.

Under "Cover Image", click "Choose File" and select your cover. Smashwords require your cover image to be a: "JPEG or PNG file. Image should be at least 1,400 pixels wide with a height greater than width."

Now "Select file of book to publish" by clicking "Choose File" and selecting your prepared EPUB, which should be under 10MB in size. Read and agree (if appropriate) to the publishing agreement and click "Publish".

Smashwords will now take some time to convert your book, and once it is ready, you will be able to see it in your Dashboard. Hopefully it will have passed the review process first time, if not follow their instructions and "Upload new version".

You will also need an ISBN to enable Smashwords to distribute your book. You can buy them from Nielsen in the UK, or Bowker in the US. Alternatively, Smashwords can assign you a free ISBN through your dashboard, listing you as the author and Smashwords as the publisher.

To obtain a Smashwords ISBN or register your existing ISBN, click on "ISBN Manager" in your dashboard and select the appropriate ISBN option. Either type in your own ISBN or copy and paste their free ISBN to your copyright page, then re-upload the revised, rechecked and reconverted file.

Once you have passed the initial reviews, it will then take some time to go through their Premium Catalogue checks. Once your book has passed this, it will be distributed to all the other sites.

3. CreateSpace

https://www.createspace.com/

i) Creating Your Account

Either sign in or sign up for an account and fill in your personal and bank account details plus tax information under "Account".

In here you will need to complete your bank account details, including bank name, branch name, IBAN (International Bank Account Number) and SWIFT/BIC code if you live outside the US. If these are not printed on your bank statements, you can find them by ringing your bank or calling into your branch. You will need to complete these details, including your tax information (see end of section) before pressing that publish button.

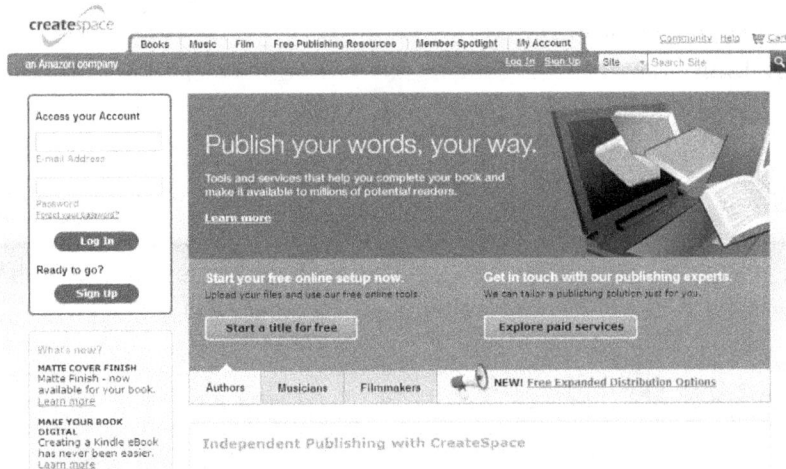

ii) Interior

The next step is to "Add New Title" from your dashboard, then you will be asked to give the title of your book and type of project. I have created a new "Working Title" book to use as an example throughout this section:

Once you have completed the details, click "Get Started" on the guided process to take you to the next screen:

Here, complete your author details, the series details if applicable, edition number, language and publication date. If you leave the publication date blank, CreateSpace will automatically use the date your book goes live. Then click "Save & Continue".

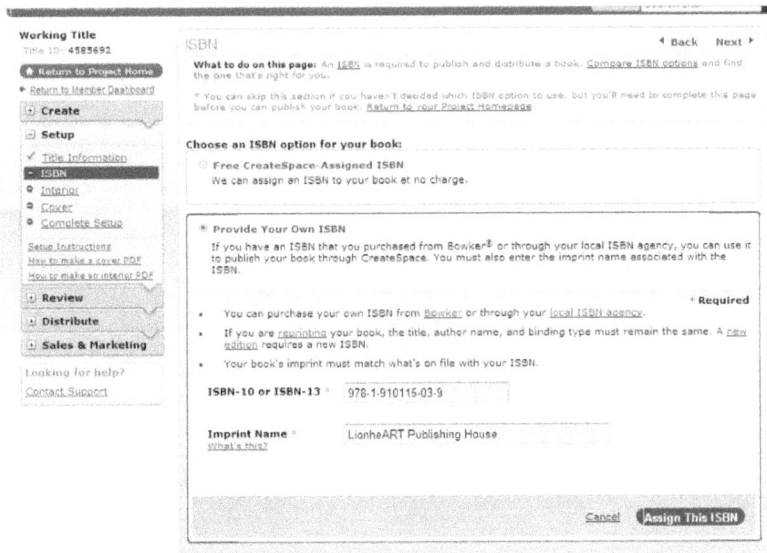

If you have bought an ISBN from Nielsen or Bowker, select "Provide Your Own ISBN" and fill in the number and Imprint Name, then click "Assign this ISBN". Alternatively click on "Free CreateSpace Assigned ISBN" which will list you as the author and CreateSpace as the publisher. Don't forget to add this ISBN to the copyright page in your Word file then reconvert to pdf.

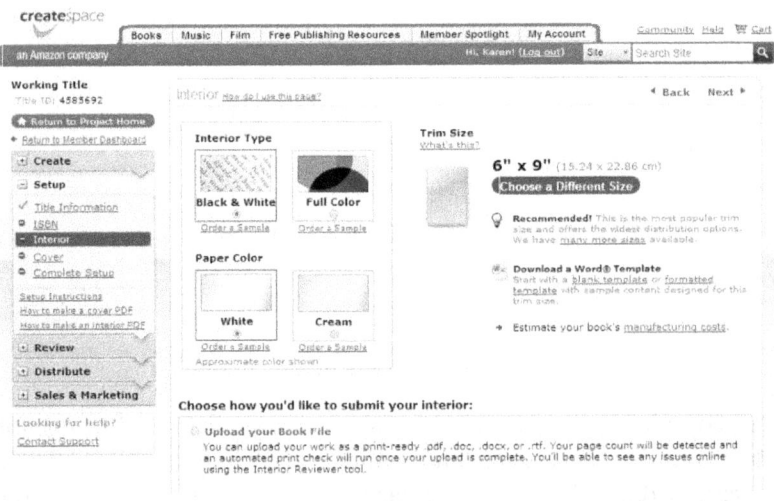

Now choose your book size, choose the "Upload your Book File" option, click "Browse", select your file and click "Save". CreateSpace will now take a few moments to upload your file then give you an option to "Launch Interior Viewer".

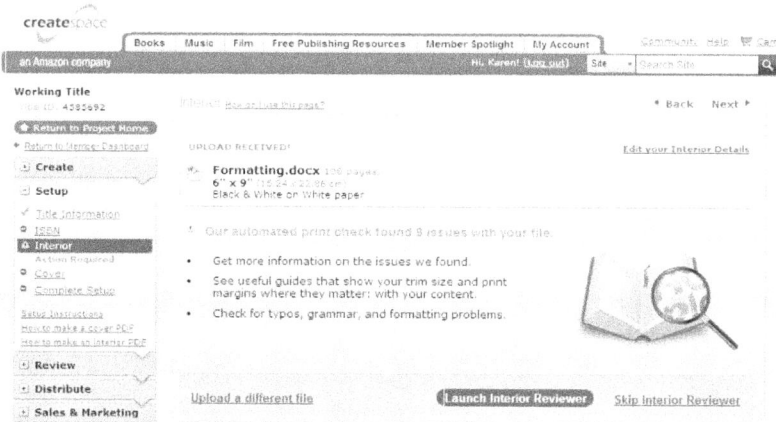

Click on this to launch the viewer to check your final format. This will also highlight any issues in your file (I have uploaded an early, unformatted draft of this book to demonstrate).

Click on "Get Started" to open the viewer:

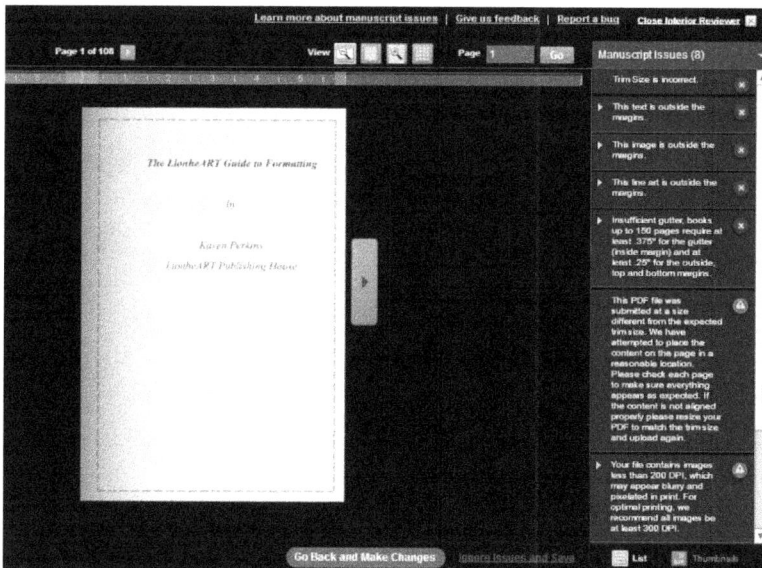

Any issues will be listed on the right-hand side. Work your way through them, amending your Word file and reconverting to pdf, then "Go Back and Make Changes", upload the revised file and re-launch the interior viewer.

If your page numbers show up as small squares in the interior reviewer, this is most likely to be due to the font used. Either use a standard font such as Times New Roman, or embed fonts as described earlier.

This time I have uploaded a fully formatted book to demonstrate:

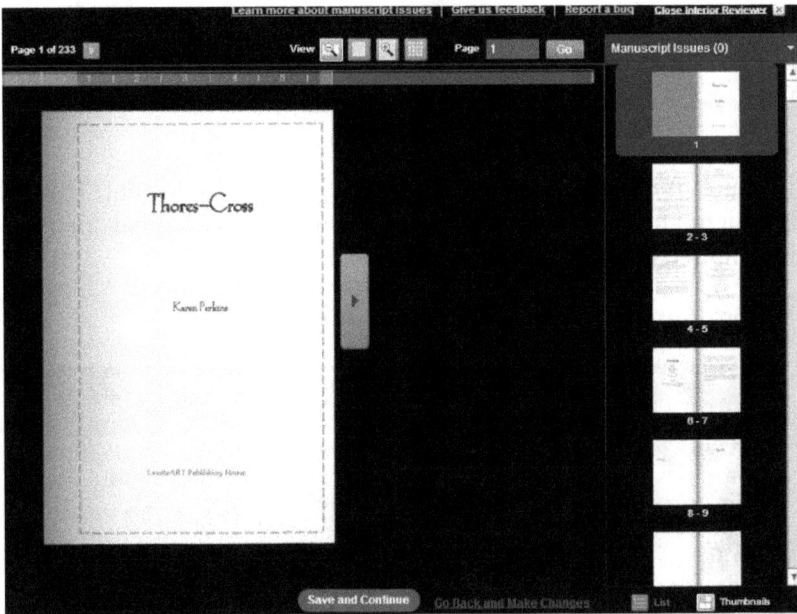

You will now have an image of your book on the left, with thumbnails of all your pages on the right. Scroll through every page of your book to ensure you are happy with the layout, click "Save and Continue", then "Continue" on the "Interior" screen.

<u>iii) Cover</u>

Once you have formatted your manuscript, let your cover designer know the page count and he or she can then prepare a paperback cover spread pdf with a correctly sized spine, ready to upload straight to CreateSpace.

CreateSpace do offer a template option, but these are easily recognizable as self-publishing templates and I do recommend having a professional cover designer prepare the format as well as design.

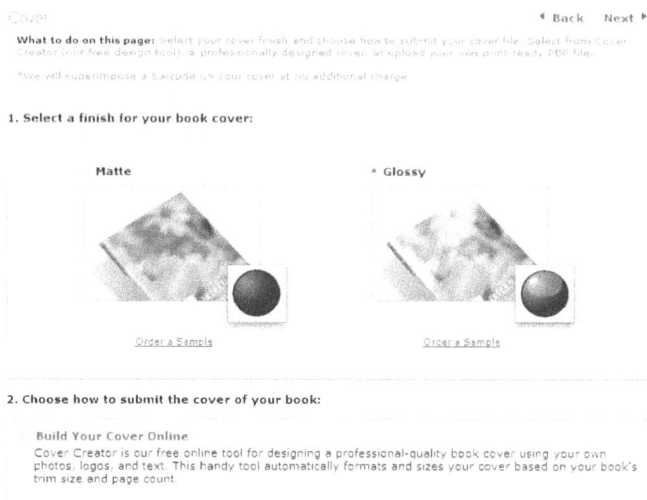

Choose whether you would like a matte or glossy finish, then click on "Upload a Print-Ready PDF Cover" and select the appropriate file.

When you are finished, click "Submit Cover" then "Complete Cover". You will then be asked to submit your files for review.

This process usually takes a day and, if everything has passed, you will then be offered proofing options. You can order a hard copy to check before publishing, which is worth taking the time to do as it is often easier to spot errors in the printed version than on screen. The colours of the cover can also print differently. In the meantime, complete your distribution page (CreateSpace now offers extended distribution for free) which will make your book available as widely as possible, then your pricing page. Finally complete the Description page:

This will affect how the Amazon page for your book will look and comprises of book description, category, author biography, book language, country of publication and search keywords.

Tick "Contains Adult Content" to avoid your book being marketed to children if it is not suitable for youngsters, and you also have an option for "Large Print".

When you click on "Save & Continue" you will then be asked if you want to publish on Kindle. CreateSpace will convert your book for Kindle, but I strongly advise you not to utilize this option as it is an automated process and will result in untidy formatting.

Once you have been notified that your proofs are ready to order, check your book very carefully before clicking the "Approve and Publish" button, then your paperback will be available on Amazon within forty eight hours. Congratulations!

British Library

Once your print book is published in the UK, you have a legal responsibility to deposit a copy with the British Library (http://www.bl.uk/aboutus/legaldeposit/printedpubs/depositprinte dpubs/deposit.html), and the ALDL (Agency for the Legal Deposit Libraries) (http://www.legaldeposit.org.uk/index.html) may also request up to five copies of your book so that a record is kept of all publications in the UK.

If you are publishing in the US, then do check out the Library of Congress website for details of requirements and copyright registration.

4. Tax

Whichever country you live in, you will need to file a tax return for your author earnings. It's therefore imperative you keep receipts and bank statements – not only for your royalties but also your expenses which can be offset against your earnings. This includes books you buy, e-readers, computer equipment, stationery etc. as well as a portion of your heating and lighting bills if you write at home. If you are in any doubt about how to keep accounts and what counts as a business expense, then do consult an accountant or bookkeeper.

If you live outside the US, Amazon (including both KDP and CreateSpace) and Smashwords will withhold 30% tax, but the US has a tax treaty with many countries worldwide, including the UK (for a full list click on: http://www.irs.gov/Businesses/International-Businesses/United-States-Income-Tax-Treaties---A-to-Z).

To change the withholding rate to 0%, you will need to telephone the IRS in the USA on 001 (267) 941-1099 (remembering the time difference). They will take some personal information from you – full name and mailing address etc. then give you an EIN (Employer Identification Number) – this is the correct number, despite the label of 'Employer'.

Input this to the tax details section of your accounts, and you can then continue and publish your book.

You will then need to complete a form W8 (which you can download from http://www.irs.gov/pub/irs-pdf/fw8ben.pdf) and send it to Amazon (and Smashwords if you have published with them too), quoting your CreateSpace Member ID – which you can find on your Member Dashboard – and your KDP Publisher's Code – which you can find by clicking on 'Your Account', it's listed quite a way down the page on the right-hand side:

Reviews

Thank you for buying and reading this formatting guide. If you found it useful, please consider leaving a rating and review on the site where you bought it. All genuine comments and feedback are extremely important to Karen Perkins and are very welcome. Thank you.

If you have any questions about formatting manuscripts that have not been covered in this guide, please do not hesitate to contact Karen Perkins on publishing@lionheartgalleries.co.uk and she will be very pleased to help you.

About the Author

Karen Perkins is the international award-winning and bestselling author of six fiction titles in the Valkyrie Series of Caribbean pirate adventures and the Yorkshire Ghost Stories. All of her fiction has appeared at the top of bestseller lists on both sides of the Atlantic with over 200,000 downloads so far.

Her first Yorkshire Ghosts novel – *Thores-Cross* – is a silver medal winner for European Fiction in the 2015 Independent Publisher Book Awards, and *Dead Reckoning: A Caribbean Pirate Adventure* reached the top 50 in the UK Kindle chart as part of *The Hot Box* set that also included work by international bestselling thriller authors David Leadbeater, John Paul Davis and Steven Bannister.

See more about Karen Perkins, including contact details, on her websites:
www.lionheartgalleries.co.uk
www.karenperkinsauthor.com

Karen is on Social Media:

Facebook:
www.facebook.com/LionheartPublishing
www.facebook.com/Yorkshireghosts
www.facebook.com/ValkyrieSeries

Twitter:
@LionheartG

Books By Karen Perkins

Non-Fiction

The LionheART Guide To Editing Fiction, UK Edition
(Available as e-book and paperback)
The LionheART Guide To Editing Fiction, US Edition
(Available as e-book and paperback)

The LionheART Guide To Formatting
(Paperbacks, Epubs and Kindle) – Available in paperback

The LionheART Guide to Formatting Paperbacks
(Available as e-books)
The LionheART Guide to Formatting EPUBs
(Available as e-books)
The LionheART Guide to Formatting for Kindle
(Available as e-books)

**To find out more about the full range of LionheART
Publishing Guides, please visit:
www.karenperkinsauthor.com/lionheart**

Fiction

Yorkshire Ghost Stories – Available as e-books and paperback
Knight of Betrayal
Thores-Cross
Cursed (short story)

To find out more about the full range of books in the Yorkshire Ghost Series, including upcoming titles, please visit:
www.karenperkinsauthor.com/yorkshire-ghosts

Valkyrie Series
Look Sharpe!
Ill Wind
Dead Reckoning

The Valkyrie Series: The First Fleet (Look Sharpe!, Ill Wind & Dead Reckoning)

Where Away – a FREE Valkyrie short story (see below)

To find out more about the full range of books in the Valkyrie Series, including upcoming titles, please visit:
www.karenperkinsauthor.com/valkyrie

Where Away is being offered FREE for readers of the Valkyrie Series and will not be released separately—if you would like to read it, please order your copy from Karen's website:
www.karenperkinsauthor.com/valkyrie

Bibliography

https://kdp.amazon.com/kdp/self-publishing/signin
https://www.smashwords.com/
https://www.createspace.com/

Coker M (2008-2013) Smashwords Style Guide:
(https://www.smashwords.com/books/view/52)

Kindle Direct Publishing: Building Your Book For Kindle:
http://www.amazon.com/Building-Your-Kindle-Direct-Publishing-
ebook/dp/B007URVZJ6/